THE VILLAGERS PRESENT
GARDENS OF MIAMI

THE VILLAGERS PRESENT
GARDENS OF MIAMI

INTRODUCTION BY JOANNA LOMBARD
PHOTOGRAPHY BY STEVEN BROOKE
TEXT BY ELAINE MILLS and JULIE PETRELLA ARCH

First published in the United States of America in 2016 by
The Villagers, Inc. Miami, Florida

ISBN-13 978-0-980-1212-1-6
Library of Congress Control Number: 2016930089
© 2016 The Villagers, Inc.

Text © 2016
by Joanna Lombard, Elaine Mills and Julie Petrella Arch

Photography © Steven Brooke

Designed by Steven Brooke Studios
Edited by Julie Petrella Arch and Donna Fields

Distributed in the United States by
The Villagers, Inc.
P.O. Box 141843
Coral Gables, FL 33114-1843
www.thevillagersinc.org

Printed and bound in the United States

COVER Waterfall from *"Old World Elegance."*
HALF-TITLE PAGE *Orchids from "Uninhibited Fun."*
TITLE PAGE Pond from *"Tropical Colors."*
RIGHT *Bamboo from "Deco Inspired."*

CONTENTS

SPONSORS

GARDEN MASTERS

SPONSORSHIP OF THE FRONT COVER
Sandy McCarthy

SPONSORSHIP OF THE TITLE PAGE AND BACK COVER
Arthur H. Hertz

HEDGE FUNDERS
CHAPTER SPONSORS

Gayle and Fuller Duncan

Marta N. Fernandez

Joanne Feuerman

Dennis Jenkins and Sunny McLean

Loyda Lewis

Bill and Linda Randolph
In memory of Dr. James Jude and Mr. David Ziska.

LANDSCAPE ARTISTS
SPONSORSHIP OF
FULL PAGE PHOTOGRAPHS

Trish and Dan Bell

Brunetti Foundation

Mary Beth Burke

Bev Gerald

Walter D. Haynes
In Memory of Gaye Grentner Haynes

Susanne Kayyali

Beverly Loftus

Dolly MacIntyre

Mongomery Botanical Center

Juan Mullerat and Megan McLaughlin
In Honor of Our Daughters, Margarita and Rose.

Thane Malison

Laura Mullaney

Ramon Pacheco

Patch of Heaven Gardens

Roe and Penny Stamps

Andrew Ware

Claire-Frances Whitehurst

GREEN THUMBS

Jean Adams
Ann Brody
Karen Buchsbaum
Casa Serena, Coconut Grove
Lynn and Lisa W. Chaffin
Charity Service Centers
Bill and Barbara Burdette
Malinda Cleary
Helen Duncan
Marlin Ebbert
Holly B. Evans
Joseph L. Falk
Historic Preservation Association of
Coral Gables
Ginger Jochem
Maria Conchita and Mario R. Lopez
Patricia Mederos
Elizabeth Muraro
Margie Palmer
Irene Priess
Charles P. Sacher
Savino and Miller Design Studio
Maxine Wishart
Mark Worsdale and Elizabeth Bolander
Wendy Angola Zepernick

FLOWER LOVERS

Karen and Henry Alexander
Julie Petrella Arch
Georgette Ballance
Bell Landscape Architecture, Inc.
Deena Bell, ASLA
Renee Betancourt
Rick and Fran Blake
Kathleen Bowker
Jeanne Bunten
David and Mercedes Carlson
Nancy Terrell Elsas
Robert Fuchs-RF Orchids
Janet P. Gardiner
Diane Lee
Becky Roper Matkov
Barbara Moller
Dr. Carmen Ortiz
Louise Petrine
Sheila W. Revell
Carolyn Reyes
Mr. and Mrs. Frank Rodriguez
Roberta Rosenberger
Howard and Carol Rubinson
Lorraine Sheldon
Kate and Lawrence Terry
Cookie Thelen
Marie Vacca
Gloria M. Villa
Martha and Frank Voytek
Joan Wieser
Linda Zahler
Julie O. Ziska
In loving memory of David L. Ziska.
Anonymous

LEAF LOVERS

Cristina Anido
Claude Augustin
Joanna Gaines Barusch
Sheila Wallace Beebe
Renee J. Belair
Louise F. Bennett
Joan Bounds
Mari Brauzer
Carola Bravo
Carol Brock
Victoria Champion
Pat Clarke
Coral Gables Garden Club
Liz Cozad
Joseph H. Deary
Lois Randall Diamond
The Dudeks
Cristina Duenas
Alexis Ehrenhaft
Sweet Pea Ellman
Andrea England
Monica Fidel
Monica Fitzgerald
Linda Flores
Anita Friedlander
Toni DeCamp Garcia
Janet R. Green
Heather and Mike Harris
Donna Hennessy
Linda Collins Hertz*
Jeanne Heyward
Verna Hodges
Jane Thurmond Holguin
Bonnie Hutton
Carole Johnson*
Sherry Jordan
Sallye Jude
Dr. Nilza Kallos
Kathleen Slesnick Kauffman
Debbie Kavanaugh
Amy Kilborne

Diane Klemick
Barbara J. Lange
Nicole Lebon-Scagnelli
Craig E. Leen, City Attorney
Lee Lennon
Judy Mangasarian
Jo Mauk
Margaret McCaffery
Susan Montesino
Joan Manda Mueller
Lou and Janet Nostro
Jane Allen Petrick
Judy Pruitt
Pauline (Polly) E. Ramos
John and Jan Sauvigne
Margaret Seroppian
Carol and John Shabe
Susan G. Shelley
Carol Keels Stanfill
Christy Starr-Klevan
Martha Stockhausen
Olga Suarez
Eva A. Swift
Carlisle Talbot
Fred and Kate Taylor
Jaye Turnbull
Kendell Turner
Ellen Uguccioni
Jody Verrengia
Lilian Walby
Rosemary Welton
Bar Werner
Carolyn C. White
Dave and Maggie Wilson
Louan Zagarino
Dr. Dee Zell
Nora Zinn
In memory of Liz Juerling.

DEDICATION

W̲E DEDICATE THIS BOOK to Frances 'Dolly' MacIntyre with respect, love and admiration. As a charter member of The Villagers, Inc., she continues to be a driving and guiding force for historic preservation and the environment. Dolly had long envisioned creating an inspirational and informative book that would share, in photographs and text, gardens such as those featured on the annual tour. This book was born of her vision. We are honored and privileged to have helped see her vision to fruition.

ACKNOWLEDGMENTS

T̲HE VILLAGERS, INC. is a non-profit organization which preserves and restores historic structures and supports the education process necessary to accomplish these efforts. Over the past five decades, almost every public site in Miami-Dade County has received some form of assistance from The Villagers. One important source of funding has been the proceeds from the organization's Spring Garden Tour, an annual event for over 25 years. The year 2016 marks the 50th anniversary of the organization.

Dolly MacIntyre and Julie Petrella Arch served as Co-Chairs for the book project, which became part of the 50th Anniversary celebration. The Villagers hoped to have such a book completely underwritten so that all proceeds would go directly to fund restoration projects, and for scholarships in the field of historic preservation. The project's Fundraising Committee, chaired by Gayle Duncan, included Carole Johnson, Beverly Loftus, Thane Malison, Linda Zahler and Julie Ziska. They accomplished their goal, thanks to the generosity of members and friends.

The first step was selecting the gardens to be included. Villager Deena Bell Llewellyn, a landscape architect, began with her own contacts in the community. Publicity Chair Karen Buchsbaum coordinated a feature article in The Miami Herald, soliciting entries for consideration. In addition to the known gardens from past tours, these efforts yielded dozens of new nominations for the book. The Selection Committee, chaired by Sheila Revell, included Karen Alexander, Renee Betancourt, Jeanne Bunten, Gayle Duncan, Bev Gerald and Deena Bell Llewellyn. The group dedicated its time to previewing properties and analyzing their merits. The goal was to represent the wide range of landscaping styles and diverse plant material in Miami-Dade County. The gardens selected run the gamut from the daringly funky to the serene, the environmentally conscious, the manicured and formal, and the truly grand. We are forever grateful to the homeowners who graciously allowed us to share their treasured gardens within the pages of this book.

Seeking the best photographer for the project, the Villagers commissioned long-time Miami resident Steven Brooke, an extensively published and internationally renowned photographer of architecture and landscape. He wholeheartedly embraced this project, providing his graphic design expertise, as well. Joanna Lombard, professor of Landscape Architecture at the University of Miami and a published author, shared her extensive knowledge and insights in the Introduction, laying the foundation and context for the gardens that follow. Writer Elaine Mills visited the chosen gardens and interviewed the owners and designers to uncover the stories behind them. Julie Petrella Arch provided additional text and botanical expertise. Villagers Barbara Moller and Judy Pruitt contributed research for the garden clubs and plant societies. Julie Petrella Arch and Donna Fields edited the book.

The Marketing Committee, including Chair Sweet Pea Ellman, Kathleen Bowker, Carole Johnson, Carolyn Reyes and Christy Starr-Klevan carried the responsibility for distribution. Other Garden Book Committee members who generously gave their time and passion to the project included Georgette Ballance, Sherry Jordan, Sallye Jude, Susanne Kayyali, Carmen Ortiz, Lilian Walby and Andrew Ware.

On behalf of all the talented people who shared their time and expertise on this project, we sincerely hope that you find genuine inspiration from the special magic and incomparable diversity of these magnificent Miami gardens.

Dolly MacIntyre and Julie Petrella Arch
Co-Chairs

The Deering Estate at Cutler, view to Biscayne Bay

INTRODUCTION
JOANNA LOMBARD

Florida is a land of illimitable light and glory, where the sun shines in splendor nearly every day throughout the livelong year, where there is no winter and the forces of nature are always active.[1]

NEARLY 100 YEARS AGO, Charles Torrey Simpson, a noted conchologist and naturalist, wrote these words in his treatise *Ornamental Gardening in Florida*. Determined to educate Floridians arriving from northern climates to the unique characteristics of Florida, particularly southern Florida, Simpson dedicated his book "To Mr. Charles Deering, who, instead of destroying the hammock, is creating it."[2] At that moment in time, Charles Deering had acquired previously platted lands around the Richmond Inn and had begun to establish an estate with an approach to gardening much lauded by the circle of botanists and scientists he supported. Deering shared his brother James's enchantment with the native landscape which composed ninety percent of Vizcaya, and of which little remains. He eschewed the formal gardens for which Vizcaya is best known today.

In Cutler, Charles Deering placed his villa entirely amidst the natural landscapes of pine rockland, hammock and mangrove, all of which were integrated into a garden of botanical and aesthetic richness that is still with us today. Recognizing the significance of this effort, Simpson advises his readers, "fortunate enough to obtain a piece of virgin hammock," to emulate the Cutler Estate approach, to leave everything "alone for a time." He believed that only after close study, such as he engaged in with the Deerings and a pantheon of other Miami plantsmen and women, could anyone truly "see its beauties, learn to love and fully appreciate it." Finally, only when "fully acquainted with its weird attractions" could work be done. This approach he felt would ensure a cautious and loving approach, so that "a path or paths may be carefully cut through it to whatever is of most interest, always leading these trails along the lines of least resistance." [3]

Simpson hoped his book would inspire garden owners to reconsider the approach of clearing first and planting later. His strategy, that of a plant enthusiast for whom the garden is a collection of beloved friends, was very much in sync with David Fairchild, the renowned plant explorer, and creator and chief of the United States Department of Agriculture Seed and Plant Introduction Section. The year 1916 also marks the date that David and Marion Fairchild began their own garden project

at the Kampong (ABOVE), designed in collaboration with landscape architect Clarence Dean. In his reflective book, *The World Grows Round My Door*, Fairchild describes this passionate circle of luminaries who shared in the adventure of gardening in Miami. He notes the contributions of Simpson and John Kunkel Small, director of the New York Botanical Garden, and close advisor to Charles Deering, for their work to introduce and educate the public on the unique and fragile qualities of South Florida's landscape.

Readers today can appreciate the concern Small brought to his book, *From Eden to Sahara Florida's Tragedy*, in which he compared the geologic conditions and characteristic vegetation he encountered on his first travels through Florida with the subsequent conditions he found in the 1920s. The photographs of his early travels recall a very different pace of life than our experiences in these same places 100 years later. In *The World Grows Round My Door*, Fairchild describes a photograph taken during the visit of tropical fruit specialist, William E. Safford, pointing out the coming together of "a great world traveler, an outstanding botanist, a great naturalist, a landscape artist, and a plant introducer," all standing at the edge of what would become the Tamiami Trail in a "superb landscape which it had taken perhaps many thousands of years to produce and the like of which was to be found nowhere else on the planet."[4] This sensibility of both the geological time frame and the uniqueness of the landscape inspired this group to band together with landscape architect Ernest Coe in the quest to create Everglades National Park.

The group concerned themselves with the larger ecology of the peninsula, as well as the details of selecting the most appropriate plant for a backyard garden. They exalted in the wonders of the native plants and delighted in the arrival of exotic specimens. They urged their contemporaries to appreciate the unique characteristics of this fragile ecosystem, and to expand the possibilities of what could be grown here in the place where, as John Kunkel Small wrote, "the floristics of temperate, subtropics, and tropic regions not only meet, but mingle."[5] He and his colleagues believed that South Florida was a "natural history museum," which "should be preserved, not only for its beauty, but also for its educational value."[6]

Now, a century later, we can trace the imprint of Miami's early gardeners as we peruse the gardens shown here. While varying in size, character, and prospect, all of the gardens illustrate the legacy of a century of plant collecting and the re-emerging concern for preservation. The gardens also suggest the quality of life that Fairchild's recollections evoke, an enjoyment of place, and the companionship of people and plants in a congenial setting.

Together, these gardens form a compendium of the many conditions and opportunities that South Florida offers. They continue the ongoing dialogue of native and exotic plants, and begin a conversation about the future. Several of the gardens directly address the ways in which shifting conditions of temperature and water levels may transform relationships among land, water, buildings and gardens. While these gardens can serve to inspire individual gardeners to develop new ideas, it is also possible that the gardens may inspire a neighborhood to consider creating a hammock or rockland in its midst, or to share in gardens that filter storm water.

The range of dimensions and plant materials also present a panorama of garden design, from intimate courtyards to expansive estates and extend to habitat restorations. The gardens revel in the tiniest of native orchids as well as the planting of some of the grandest of exotic tropical trees. Drawing upon the abundance of riches established through the horticultural explorations and educational programs of Fairchild Tropical Botanic Garden as well as the numerous, informed and dynamic plant societies, each garden seeks its own identity through the plant communities it celebrates.

Vizcaya Museum and Gardens

Fairchild Tropical Botanic Garden

As diverse as the gardens are, they also share themes that are fundamental and unique to South Florida. The celebration of oolitic limestone is consistently present, although the role of limestone in the garden varies from stair risers that form thin ribbons across a lawn, to the foundations of buildings that appear to be rising from the limestone shelf upon which the community is perched, to highly detailed and ornately carved gates and figures. Many of the distinctive selections of plant material and position share an attentiveness to the microclimates of the gardens so that plantings are chosen for compatibility with specific waterfront exposures, or in an inland garden, the breezes across a patio, or the humidity laden air of a poolside grotto.

Each garden also presents to the visitor a highlight that gives a memorable identity significant to its place. This may be a particular element that inspires contemplation, a powerful presence. For some of the gardens, that presence is found in the use of water, either through the prospect of the horizon across Biscayne Bay, the reflection of the sky in pools and fountains, or the sound of water falling over an edge and into a pool. For other gardens, a singular landscape element, a formidable *Ficus aurea*, or a spectacular baobab, anchors the relationship of the house and garden. The highlight can also be a comprehensive experience, such as winding through a hammock, or experiencing the recreation of a pine rockland in the middle of the city. When distance, water, or major specimen trees are too large for the

space, the garden can direct the eye upward, to what Frank Button, George Merrick's landscape designer of Coral Gables, identified as "the most important adjunct to the landscape artist," South Florida's "wonderful blue sky with masses of snowy clouds lightly floating." Button focused on the potential for landscape to frame the magical moment when "at sunset the day passes, through all the liquid colors of the rainbow, into a brilliant starry night."[7] One can imagine the air redolent with the scents of the tropical flowering plants which fill the small alcoves, grottoes and courtyard gardens.

This broad range of garden experiences illustrates the unifying aspect of long-standing design principles associated with South Florida. The focused vista of the night sky from within the luxuriant foliage of a secluded court, for example, illustrates the principle of contrast that William Lyman Phillips, designer of Fairchild Tropical Botanic Garden, identified as one of three aspects, unity, contrast, and variety, essential to garden design. A graduate of the class of 1910, among the ranks of early alumni from Harvard's Landscape Architecture program, Phillips studied with Frederick Law Olmsted, Jr., the son of renowned American Landscape Architect Fredrick Law Olmsted, and a noted designer in his own right. The Olmsted office projects generally adhered to the idea that a landscape should be memorable, in that a visitor should be able to leave the garden with a concept of the place well formed in the mind. This typically called for a design that could be

Crandon Park

read, in the sense that a landscape would reveal itself to the visitor through a unifying strategy such as a grand vista or central organizing axis that produces a sense of wholeness. Then, as the visitor explored, the landscape would provide a series of inviting discoveries through the two principles of contrast and variety. When experienced in total, these events of the garden would build to a larger understanding of place, a unity which firmly embeds the memory of the garden in the mind and heart of the visitor.

Phillips applied this strategy to the parks and gardens he designed throughout South Florida, most notably the Heritage Parks of Miami Dade County, in which the individual parts of each landscape contribute in various ways to a harmonious whole.[8] In the larger gardens presented here, the visitor experiences contrast through sunny and shady spots, overlooks and grottoes. Variety is found in the changing relationships of spaces and walkways, near and far views, plant materials, colors, and textures.

These principles are evident in gardens of all sizes. An estate garden, for example, introduces passages through tree-lined walkways that yield to a sunny, sunken lawn. A pool garden contrasts the clean geometry of a parterre's edge with a bed of raucous plants. On a larger scale, oolitic limestone cut smooth in a formal terrace transitions to a rough-hewn face as it moves to the water's edge. In a small courtyard, smooth and rough surfaces define doorways and fountain edges, respectively. The success of a garden can be measured in how well each of these elements introducing contrast

and variety builds to create a memorable place. Applying the Phillip's triad and imagining the garden in one's mind can provide the viewer with a method of analysis that unifies the gardens across the diversity of their origins and dimension.

Beyond considerations of composition and organization, each garden hosts a specific character of life. Many of the gardens offer transitional spaces in which architecturally defined terraces closer to the house transform into rustic paths at the garden's edge. This is a classic approach to garden design in which the spaces closest to the house are the most formal and geometric, serving as outdoor versions of the spaces and rooms within, an approach found in many of the early Florida gardens which focused on beneficial air flow and were important to enhancing cross-ventilation within the house. With air-conditioning, it became possible for gardens to suggest an edenic fluidity between interior and exterior space so that the house appears to float within a more densely planted landscape, an illusion that is enabled through elevated platforms and vertical separations between plantings and structures.

Between these two positions of transition and juxtaposition are gradations of indoor and outdoor spatial relationships, some of which belie the heat, humidity and insect life that are the inevitable denizens of a Florida garden. The gardens also can be explored in relation to the success with which they provide a measure of comfort—relief from the sun, access to breeze, shelter in the rain, distance from less appealing garden residents, such as snakes, which Phillips thought could be managed by designing paths that were cleared of underbrush so that a visitor might "walk without brushing against leafy vegetation and getting filled up with red-bugs."[9] These are the practical considerations of gardens that enable garden rooms to serve as active extensions of the life of the house.

As varied as they are in origin, design, and intent, the gardens collected here demonstrate a consistency of motivating spirt in that each garden contains aspects that are finely detailed to a particular purpose and location, while at the same time suggestive of a vision for the way that the larger public landscape might hold some of these elements within its grander scope. When George Merrick's team explained his vision for the gardens of Coral Gables in the 1920s, they noted that, "it takes but a little while in this zone of equable climate for garden beauty to spring to attractiveness, and the years but bring perfection."[10] The gardens we see here point to a potential for the region that represents the best of our past, as well as hopes for our future, perhaps not perfection, but certainly a vision of life in all its beauty and possibility.

Royal poinciana on Old Cutler Road

NOTES

[1]Charles Torrey Simpson, *Ornamental Gardening in Florida: A Treatise on the Decorative Plants Adapted to Florida and Their Cultivation, With Suggestions for the Ornamentation of Florida Homes and Grounds,* Little River, Florida, 1916:39. http://www.biodiversitylibrary.org/bibliography/19808#/summary

[2]Simpson, 1916, frontispiece.

[3]Simpson, 1916, 4.

[4]David Fairchild, *The World Grows Round My Door,* New York and London: Charles Scribner's Sons, 1947: 57-59.

[5] John Kunkel Small, *From Eden to Sahara Florida's Tragedy,* Lancaster, PA: The Science Press Printing Company, 1929: 114. http://ufdc.ufl.edu/UF00055168/00001/139j

[6]Small, Ibid. 114.

[7]Frank Button, "Landscaping in Southern Florida," Southern Architect and Building News, February 1930: 71.

[8]William Lyman Phillips, "The Fairchild Tropical Garden: A Memoir," 3 September 1958, page 8. file 13-1:4, William Lyman Phillips Papers, Charlton W. Tebeau Library of Florida History, HistoryMiami.

[9]William Lyman Phillips to Waldo E. Sexton, Lake Wales, June 4, 1931, file 13-1:4, *William Lyman Phillips Papers,* Charlton W. Tebeau Library of Florida History, HistoryMiami.

[10]*Typical Gardens of Coral Gables* (n.p.: Parker Art Printing Association, c.1920s) 3.

DECO INSPIRED

An ART DECO-STYLE home built in 1939 on Miami Beach, designed by Russell Pancoast, has been lovingly restored to former glory, with garden and outdoor living areas as important as its interiors. The owners are enthusiastic gardeners who do most of the plant installation and maintenance themselves. Their horticultural consultant, Randall A. Kalember, helps them source rare and unusual plants.

The property is divided into five distinct areas: a street garden, Florida garden, rainforest, Balinese garden and a lake garden.

An elegant Art Deco gateway is centered within the street garden. This mulched area is filled with palms, colorful bromeliads and a variety of native plant material, requiring little or no maintenance. This garden is a more environmentally conscious alternative to the traditional sodded front lawn. The thick planting of trees and shrubs helps prevent the heat of the road surface from radiating into the adjacent rainforest.

The rainforest garden is a dense tangle of rare palms and orchids, anchored by the lone original tree, a prized mamey sapote. Oaks were planted to provide shade and structure. The straight limestone entry path becomes a meander through this lush area, inspired by travel to Costa Rica. Many of the rarest palms in this part of the yard are endangered or imperiled in their native habitats.

Also leading from the street garden through a smaller yet matching gate, is the Florida garden, a charming sitting area filled with found objects, butterfly plants and sunshine. The Florida and rainforest gardens are enclosed in a low masonry wall cloaked in creeping fig vine, providing privacy and background for the abundant street-side planting.

Beyond the rainforest, the Balinese garden, designed by Savino & Miller Design Studios, offers a lush setting for more rare palms, surrounding a water garden with a central limestone terrace and stepping stones that appear to float above the fish and water lilies. A stunning carved stone Art Deco door frame rescued from demolition in Chicago has been repurposed as a

waterfall and focal point. This garden's sitting area has become the central living room, accessible from both wings of the home, with views to Surprise Lake beyond. The blend of styles and materials is most apparent here, unified by the deep green vegetation and accented by colorful orchids and crotons chosen for their butter yellow color to match the stone.

The lake garden offers a serene view from the covered patio, over the pool and waterside dining deck to Surprise Lake. A simple stone coping and minimal lawn panels surround the pool, providing a multi-purpose space to entertain and relax. This deck is a favorite spot for watching dolphin and manatee.

LEFT *One of two Chicago Art Deco remnants.*

ABOVE *A 'found' gate inspired the new Art Deco gateway that leads from the street into the rainforest.*

TOP *View toward rainforest garden.*

ABOVE *View across Florida room sitting area to another rescued Art Deco cornice. Potted chrysanthemums, bromeliads and bird-of-paradise* (Strelitzia reginae) *frame the sitting area.*

RIGHT *Close-up of single 'found' settee.*

FACING ABOVE *A companion gateway leads from the drive to the Florida garden room.*

FACING BELOW LEFT *Bromeliads line a walkway to the front gate.*

FACING BELOW RIGHT *Simple detailing and subtle colors match the home's interior, and compliment the vibrant foliage.*

FACING ABOVE *The arch has been fitted with a fountain that pours down over white water lilies* (Nymphaea odorata).

FACING BELOW *The Balinese garden viewed through a Lau fan palm* (Pritchardia thurstonii), *a rare palm from eastern Fiji.*

ABOVE *Lakeside pool garden and patio.*

RIGHT *Evening in the Balinese-style garden.*

OLD WORLD ELEGANCE

IN A BLEND OF OLD WORLD formality and New World tropical abundance, this expansive Coconut Grove garden offers a variety of settings to enjoy the natural world. The arches, symmetry and paving patterns of Tuscan villas inspired the home and garden's formal areas. Use of local coral rock, still and running water, winding paths through dense native plantings, and changes in elevation combine to create a place of boundless beauty, at peace within its South Florida environs. The historic Mediterranean Revival home was designed in 1924 and acquired by its current owners in 2001. At a substantial four acres, a garden of this size is a true luxury for this area of Miami-Dade County.

In the summer of 2005, three successive hurricanes destroyed much of the property's original landscape. Seeing which plants survived suggested to the landscape architect, Raymond Jungles, a new landscape design with lower maintenance native plants, accented by rare palms. Dense plantings provide privacy between various garden rooms. The journey from the formality of the house and immediate surroundings to a sultry jungle space at garden's end is an enchanting adventure.

Inspired by their trips to Italy, the owners created a magnificent coral rock archway that frames the entrance to a large formal garden with reflecting pool and dining pavilion. The pool is flanked by a symmetrical arrangement of large potted blue agave, lawn panels that are frequently graced by preening neighborhood peacocks, and arcades of coral rock arches. This part of

the garden also features antique sculptures, fountains and glass lanterns collected from around the world, and contemporary sculptures by artist and friend, Michele Oka Doner.

The archways of the Italian garden draw visitors through the formal setting toward more casual pavilions near the swimming pool, along winding paths, past ponds and waterfalls, up and down stairways built into lush hills, and over numerous bridges. Visitors are treated to a kaleidoscope of sounds, textures, colors and fragrances. Private sitting areas are interspersed with areas for dining and gathering.

Mosaic pebble pavement weaves throughout the garden like a richly textured carpet. It transitions to a tapestry of cut coral rock around the swimming pool,

then irregular coral pavers, and ultimately mulch, as the lush jungle seems to overtake the garden's far reaches. These paths transport visitors through a sequence of garden rooms, evoking the sense of a classic stroll garden.

ABOVE LEFT *A graceful stairway begins the descent toward the deep garden.*

ABOVE *Archways of smooth and rough-cut limestone, rich with coral fossils, frame many lovely vistas. Chalice vine (Solandra grandiflora) above this archway from the motor court, framed by silver date palm (Phoenix sylvestris).*

FOLLOWING *This dining pavilion's setting was inspired by Moorish gardens of Spain and Tuscan villas of Italy, with arches, tile roofs and symmetrical arrangements of date palms, potted century plant, low-clipped hedging and lawn panels.*

LEFT *Twin arcades of archways lead from either side of the formal garden toward the natural garden rooms. Lined with towering bamboo and gravel walks, breezes and footsteps compliment the sounds of the birds.*

TOP *A pair of carved stone lion thrones flank the archway just inside the formal garden.*

ABOVE *The carpet-like pebble mosaic of the entry court forms a lovely welcome mat. The giant fronds of the oil palms that flank the doorway can be 30 feet or more in length, forming impressive vase shaped sentries that anchor the landscape.*

FACING TOP
FACING TOP
Near the residence, a swimming pool wraps around the adjacent cabana – a setting designed for relaxing and entertaining.

FACING
BELOW LEFT
Favorite orchids are tucked among palms and philodendron.

FACING
BELOW RIGHT
Vandaceous orchids hang from trees.

TOP
Limestone path leading to the deep garden pond, lined with 'Green Island' ficus, philodendron and a vast collection of rare palms and cycads. Dangling pothos vines add to the impression of mystery ahead.

MIDDLE
An artfully meandering path of irregular limestone pavers, edged with mondo grass. The spiky, double-trunked zombie palm, on the left, offers striking contrast to the concrete-like trunks of the Bailey's copernicia palm in the distance.

BELOW
View from above waterfall within the deep garden, toward the Florida thatch palm that marks the entrance. The stained-glass effect of the variegated pothos leaves brightens this large, intensely green grotto.

A mesh armature draped over the sculptural walls of the deep garden supports a magnificent array of foliage, including a dark green, fan-shaped Bailey's copernicia palm (Copernicia baileyana).

LEFT
A flight of curving stairs descends to the lowest level of the garden – an intimate seating area within the deep garden grotto, near the waterfall. The pebble mosaic paving continues the connection to the formal areas.

RIGHT
One of several waterfalls emerging from dense greenery in this multilevel garden.

TOP *View of the main waterfall, which provides cooling sound and mist throughout much of the deep garden.*

ABOVE *View across the deep garden from surrounding stairs and paths.*

RIGHT *A carpet of pebble mosaic draws visitors from the informal garden toward the formal, along a lovely Mediterranean-style fountain basin. Lady palms and creeping fig line the narrow corridor.*

FOLLOWING *Dramatic night time view of the deep garden and waterfalls. The curly trunk fibers of the Cuban old man palm* (Coccothrinax crinita) *at left, above broad leaves of Swiss cheese plant* (Monstera deliciosa).

CONSERVING THE WILDERNESS

WITH EXCEPTIONAL SENSITIVITY and commitment to conservation, the owners of this South Dade Redland paradise are establishing a haven for themselves and for local wildlife. Inspired by Miami's unspoiled origins and a driving force to help steward the future, this approximately 20-acre work in progress includes preservation of an existing house and tropical hardwood forest, and extension of the habitat on adjacent county -owned land. The project is overseen by resident horticulturalist Frederick Hubbard.

The home is entirely integrated with the land; water is a central theme with ponds, pools and waterfalls creating a soothing habitat for humans and wildlife. Feeding the koi fish in their pond is one of the owners' favorite pastimes, as is sighting animals, which include a pair of great horned owls that appear now year after year.

A large portion of the property is protected hardwood hammock forest, with some areas restricted from any type of disturbance, and others subject to strict rules governing removal of invasive species, restoration of native plants and ongoing management plans. Portions of the land formerly used as plant nurseries offer the greatest possibilities for creative transformation. Several areas will be converted over time to pine rockland and Everglades habitat; others are being planted with a variety of fruit trees as an experiment in agroforestry.

The lawn adjacent to the house is anchored by a large Florida strangler fig (*Ficus aurea*) with the view terminating at a magnificent royal poinciana (*Delonix regia*), endemic to the western forests of Madagascar, but long an iconic tree of South Florida. Several planting beds surround this lawn, providing a setting for woodland stump furniture seating groups and a whimsical collection of giraffe sculptures that appear to graze on the vegetation.

With an extraordinary vision for a long and fruitful legacy, the owners established an area as a model of sustainable agroforestry. Rock from excavations on the property was used to create a formal, terraced allée for *Theobroma cacao* trees that will be sheltered from occasional cold by using interplanting techniques. A large statue of Buddha stands at the end of the allée where it will eventually appear to emerge from a tangle of trees, vines and ferns.

The owners hope eventually to establish a model processing facility on the property to make artisanal chocolate from their cacao trees. They have sourced their plants from Fairchild Tropical Botanic Garden's member and plant society sales, and the Connect to Protect Network, which preserves globally endangered pine rocklands. Experts from Fairchild, the USDA and Miami-Dade County are among the numerous resources providing advice on agroforestry and habitat restoration. Ultimately, in heart and mind, these naturalists hope to create an educational foundation based on a sustainable model that can inspire others, regardless of their property's size or their resources.

LEFT *Gateway with intricately carved creatures, fashioned from the roots of a lychee tree* (Litchi chinensis).

ABOVE *A resting place beneath the Florida strangler fig* (Ficus aurea).

FACING TOP *Pathway leading into formerly open nursery grounds.*
Trees planted as small nursery stock grow quickly to create the desired jungle effect.

FACING MIDDLE *Fountain surrounded by terraced limestone excavated during creation of the pond.*

FACING BELOW *Lush pathway to pond.*

ABOVE *In this manmade pond, koi fish have quickly grown from six inches to three feet in length. Bald cypress* (Taxodium distichum) *and giant leather fern* (Acrostichum danaeifolium) *live happily on a submerged ledge.*

TOP *An elevated sitting area with rustic stump furniture overlooks the pond, framed by clusia.*

BELOW LEFT *A wide variety of philodendron, begonias and orchids line the jungle-like pathways.*

BELOW RIGHT *Limestone blocks are quickly cloaked in ferns and moss.*

FACING TOP *The casual lounging area beside the pond is graced by a carved sandstone art panel.*

FACING BELOW *A cluster of cypress knees peek out from a moist area, beneath a giant leather fern.*

A pond-side sitting area surrounded by ferns.

A casual sitting area on the upper lawn, surrounded by a portion of the vast collection of favorite bromeliads.

Giraffe sculptures playfully placed as though nibbling on foliage.

TOP *The open lawn near the homestead is sheltered by a huge strangler fig.*

ABOVE *With a cedar shake ceiling and walls of screen, interior koi pond, bridge and limestone waterfall wall, the historic home is a museum for plants, animals and beautiful artifacts.*

COCONUT GROVE EXOTIC

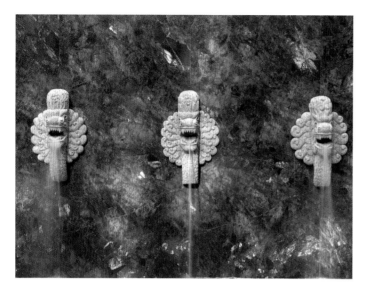

SAVING THE ENORMOUS live oak trees on this Coconut Grove property was of foremost importance during the design and construction of this home. The owner's directive to architect George S. Lopez and landscape designer Carlos Somoza was to preserve the oaks "above all else." These majestic oak trees (*Quercus virginiana*) form a canopy that covers the entire front yard and lines its motor court. Adorned with orange, magenta, yellow and white orchids, the trees also serve as a safe haven for a large group of neighborhood peacocks.

Dense groupings of ground cover and understory plantings, including native paurotis, or Everglades palms, give the appearance of well-managed fullness. A brick wall shields the house from the street and is the backdrop for the open-air garden visible through large windows lining the front of the house.

The home and garden reflect the personal style of the owner, an avid adventure traveler who has created a museum-like setting for his outstanding collection of tribal and contemporary art. Vistas from every window have been maximized, including views of the property's side yards. These corridors between the front and back yards are rich in detail. Stucco walls display a highly ornamental collection of rare staghorn ferns and colorful orchids. A small, secluded sitting area on the northeast side of the house is nestled within a bamboo-like cabada palm (*Dypsis cabadae*) forest juxtaposed against a contrasting horizontal-slat fence. Meandering light-colored limestone pavers brighten the heavily shaded space, along with a large mirror on the exterior wall that extends the view and animates the area.

The rear yard, featuring a well-appointed outdoor kitchen, pool and pavilion, is an excellent spot for entertaining and relaxation. While the heavily planted front and side yards create one type of landscape, the rear yard's large plant material is located along the property's perimeter. The airy openness in the middle of this space is a delightful contrast to other areas of the property.

The focal point of the pool patio is an unusual wall of fabulous labradorite stone, which serves as a foil for three Chinese dragon fountainheads, providing soothing sounds of falling water. Labradorite's highly refractive, iridescent properties create a blue-green opalescent shine with the changing patterns of the sun. An elevated brown marble deck provides a warm transition between the patio and glass-walled room where the owner's impressive sculptures are displayed. Another prized collection, that of rare and unusual palms, such as the Asian satake (*Satekentia liukiuensis*) palm, complements this remarkable setting.

The landscape, created with the assistance of horticulturist Debra DeMarco, is largely a study of numerous shades of green, expressed in a wide range of leaf shapes, patterns, textures and sizes, and supplemented with restrained splashes of color from blooming orchids and furnishings. Limiting the palette of colors and increasing the variety of textures has created an elegant garden that is both tranquil and vibrant. According to the owner, this garden, called Oak Garden at Silver Bluff, "celebrates what makes us different rather than the same."

LEFT *A trio of dragon head fountain spouts, carved in China, form the centerpiece of the labradorite stone feature wall.*

ABOVE *Live oaks along the front drive provide a showcase for orchids of all types.*

TOP *Side yard with limestone pavers and black river stones attractively contrast cabada palm trunks (Dypsis cabadae) and horizontal fence slats.*

ABOVE *A gallery of staghorn ferns in the side yard.*

RIGHT *Long staghorn fronds stretch toward the ground.*

FACING TOP *Paurotis palms line the front privacy wall of the home, providing a genuine South Florida ambience.*

FACING MIDDLE LEFT *Color bursts and contrasting textures brighten the elegant front privacy wall.*

FACING MIDDLE RIGHT *Colorful vanda and phalaenopsis orchids.*

FACING BOTTOM LEFT *Contrasting leaf textures and variations in green are orchestrated to great effect using large-leaved alocasia 'Lutea', giant leopard plant (Farfugium japonicum 'Giganteum') and red croton.*

FACING BOTTOM RIGHT *Sun streaming through the oaks.*

FOLLOWING PAGES *Three Cuban old man palms (Coccothrinax crinita) are featured beside the pool. Dramatic use of landscape lighting enlivens the entertainment areas.*

UNINHIBITED FUN

THIS 1930's HOME AND GARDEN have evolved over time as joyful and exuberant expressions of the owners' artistic talents and appreciation of color. In this fun and funky Coconut Grove cottage, the garden flows inside, the art flows outside, and nearly every surface and corner is treated to color, texture and lush vegetation.

Unique mosaic columns that flank the front door are set against deep red exterior walls. Created by the owners themselves, these mosaics are both a gift to the traditionally iconoclastic Coconut Grove neighborhood, and a hint at the treasures integral to the fabric of the home, both inside and out. Exceptional and rare art tiles are embedded into interior and exterior walls, sharing space with the owners' personal art works.

The heart of the home is an enclosed atrium living room with a large, uninterrupted pane of glass that gives the illusion of bringing the garden indoors. Outdoors, an abundance of plants in beds and pots surrounds cozy sitting areas.

The yard began as a forlorn lot with a sodded lawn and just one token tree. It has grown in an organic celebration of regionalism, taking inspiration from Florida, the Caribbean, Haitian and Native American cultures. Raw construction materials, such as steel reinforcing bars, support awnings, and plants create perches for birds. Plant material is used as a tool to create texture in the painted stucco surfaces. The garden is a bold expression of the owners' interests and endless creativity. Vibrant color emanates from neon-toned bromeliads and jewel-colored orchids.

Each item in this happy assemblage has a story and personal meaning, and the garden has been a constant source of joy and wonderment for its owners, who have gained much pleasure from sticking plants in the ground and just standing back. "In the end," they say, "It turned out much better than we expected!"

LEFT *Built-in shelving on exterior wall is adorned with molded Italian tiles and mirrored copper mosaic inlay.*

ABOVE *The intensely colored walls and mosaic tiles of the unique columns represent the spirit of Coconut Grove at its best.*

FOLLOWING *The back yard is crowned by a royal poinciana and colorful bougainvillea vines.*

FACING *Side yard privacy wall organically layered with plaster, paint and mirrored tile fragments.*

ABOVE *Benches and architectural remnants, artistically placed in the front courtyard.*

BELOW *Potted bromeliads and bougainvillea are bright spots in the dense green vegetation surrounding the Mexican cantera dining table.*

ABOVE *Mosaics and the metal structure were added to bring interest to a flat rear wall.*
Dragon tree (Dracaena marginata) *placed beside atrium wall allows birds and orchids to perch close to the window.*

FACING ABOVE *Rear wall of studio with mosaic and embedded art tiles.*

FACING BELOW LEFT *Heavily textured plaster and tiles with mosaic add interest to exterior wall.*

FACING BELOW RIGHT *Deep red anthuriums add an exotic quality to the plantings.*

FACING TOP *Red canvas stretched between studio wall and a tower of rebar creates a favorite spot to lounge with a book.*

FACING BELOW LEFT *Sculptural chairs behind potted caladium* (Caladium bicolor).

FACING BELOW RIGHT *Palm inflorescences were used to give texture to the plaster of the purple pergola columns. Red steel pipes are supported by massive beams of pine heartwood recovered from the Suwanee River after 60 or more years under water.*

ABOVE *The enclosed atrium brings the garden into the heart of the home. Paint patterns were inspired by Seminole Indian patchwork fabrics.*

Devotion to Beauty

A PRIVATE GARDEN RETREAT allows a glimpse into the soul of a brilliant architect whose professional work was characterized by a minimalist aesthetic of steel and glass in the tradition of Mies van der Rohe. In his own Coconut Grove cottage-style home, the minimalist aesthetic is taken to the rare extreme of entirely black building exteriors, entirely white building interiors, complemented by warm brick paving that flows from interior to exterior, drawing visitors into the garden. It is the garden that reigns supreme.

The owner said, "When I was looking for a house, I wanted a property with mature trees so I could create my garden under a fully developed canopy." With the help of his friend and landscape architect, the late Allen Fernandez, this lifelong gardener created a succession of garden rooms full of thoughtfully placed plants and pathways that create floors, walls and ceilings. Winding paths draw visitors through the dense green landscape, past towering black bamboo stems, and through gigantic clumps of ginger. Vibrant bursts of colorful orchids are seen at every level, including massive plantings mounted overhead in the sheltering oak canopy.

The pool patio forms the heart of the compound, surrounded by the carefully contained jungle. The black cottage and studio enhance the impression of limitless density. Small openings in the greenery allow glimpses of crushed coral stone paths, inviting curiosity and exploration. Despite the relatively small size of the lot, the dense foliage between the pea rock paths offers a surprising feeling of a long and interesting journey.

The interiors and the garden are in true harmony. Views from the home offer deep green vignettes with stunning splashes of color from orchids, heliconia and croton. At night, the meticulously crafted interiors are framed by the lush plantings. This gardener's true love of plants and collecting shines through in the painterly compositions found in each corner. The scale and placement of precious objects are highly considered, and the warmth and texture of the red brick patios and steps and black clapboard buildings unite the compositions.

This garden appears to block out the world with its tremendous density and the soaring verticality of a tropical rainforest. At the same time, it is a self-contained environment for the extraordinary life lived within. Dozens of Miami homeowners have taken their inspiration from this unique expression of one man's love of the pleasures of gardening.

LEFT *Dense jungle view with the epiphytic Anthony's rick-rack cactus (*Cryptocereus anthonyanus*) at upper right. This is a night-blooming cactus, whose fragrant blossoms last only a single night.*

ABOVE *View across pool to residence on left, studio on right. The entirely black facades of the buildings allow the jungle, pool and warm brick patio to take center stage. The rooster sculpture is the centurion of the pool.*

RIGHT *Careful composition of yellow vanda-ceous orchid, croton (*Codiaeum variegatum*) and lady palm (*Rhapis excelsa*).*

ABOVE *Up-lights show off the texture of the palm trunks and shine on the undersides of the Vanuatu fan palm (Licuala grandis).*

LEFT *Tropical plants, from ground to sky, give a delightful view from every angle.*

FACING ABOVE *Potted orchids, hanging begonias, and a gorgeous display of heliconia.*

FACING BELOW *The cottage is dramatically sur-rounded by the meticulously crafted jungle.*

RIGHT *Colorful bursts from massive displays of orchids.*

BELOW LEFT *Warm brick carries from the deck to the chimney to the interior floors for seamless transitions.*

BELOW MIDDLE *Casual seating beside a lovely tropical medenilla at left.*

BELOW RIGHT *A series of pea rock paths meanders through the dark jungle.*

A GARDEN FOR ART

THIS EXTRAORDINARY CORAL GABLES ESTATE, with nearly seven acres of beautiful gardens along Biscayne Bay, is surrounded on three sides by water. Elevations and depressions were cleverly sculpted to create charming settings from which to view the garden and distant horizon. The owners are avid art collectors and the landscape was carefully designed by Robert Parsley to showcase their large-scale sculptures, which are elegantly displayed for optimal viewing from the residence and grounds. Through the use of changes in topography and careful placement of dense plant material, a series of garden vignettes was created, which make this large estate seem intimate and accessible. Every tree on the estate, but for a venerable, storm-battered sea grape, was moved or brought in to complement the home and garden.

"We love to get up early and walk with the dogs around the property for exercise," say the owners who enjoy strolling the scenic, limestone path that encircles the home. A series of delightful spaces designed for entertaining and enjoying life outdoors includes a sunken garden with vine-covered pergola, an enormous waterside chickee hut with a circular bench and a La Caja China roasting box that is a popular location for gatherings. A large banyan tree fitted with African art screens and showerhead provides a refreshing antidote for long days on the water.

The swimming pool sits within a formal courtyard reminiscent of a Renaissance palazzo, complete with an elevated pavilion and outdoor kitchen. This Italianate belvedere is a romantic place to enjoy the sunset. The pool is connected to the home by terraces, stairs, and vine-covered loggias. Arching fountains jet from invis-

ible spouts in the terrace. A nearby koi pond marks the transition to a lovely garden, where a cluster of Madagascar palms, with spiny trunk and white blossoms, forms a striking centerpiece.

Large banyan trees and palms anchor the oak-lined driveway that leads to a grand rotunda at the home's main entrance. Carefully trained bougainvillea and jasmine accent the façade of the home, adding color and fragrance. Potted citrus trees, inspired by travels in Spain, decorate the many terraces.

Hammocks hung between the palm trees, Adirondack chairs and carved natural wood

benches are located throughout the many garden rooms. A promontory along the eastern seawall makes a favorite place to watch the sunrise each morning.

LEFT *One of many sculptures sited throughout the garden.*

ABOVE *Main drive, paved with warm Argentinian porphyry stone, and lined with live oaks and silver date palms, leads to a grand rotunda.*

ABOVE *Canary Island date palms (Phoenix canariensis) line the boulevard.*

FACING ABOVE *Smooth limestone pavers laid in herringbone pattern beside rough-cut limestone retaining walls.*

RIGHT *Broad walkway atop seawall leads to a favorite chair for panoramic viewing beneath the royal palms.*

FOLLOWING *Banyan tree beside the master terrace, a broad formal lawn that links the home to the water.*

BELOW *Silver date palms frame the pool and view toward the elevated cabana.*

FACING ABOVE *Spa pool with central hot tub.*

FACING MIDDLE *Sea grape and coconuts shelter a rustic waterside seating area.*

FACING BELOW *A large, circular chickee hut with kitchen/bar, and hammocks strung between coconut palms, makes an ideal location for entertaining at sunset.*

ABOVE
*"Banyan" can refer
to several species
of fig trees. The
Indian banyan (Ficus
benghalensis) is
the national tree of
India, revered for
its prop roots that,
once anchored, form
massive tree colo-
nies, as this one has
begun to develop.*

LEFT
*The banyan dwarfs
a huge rough-cut
limestone bench.*

FACING
*An African art panel
offers privacy for
this unique outdoor
shower facility.*

FOLLOWING
*Distant view of Key
Biscayne is filtered
through perimeter
plantings that offer
privacy and wind
protection. A large
staghorn fern ball
hangs from banyan.*

GABLES SPLENDOR

THIS CLASSIC MEDITERRANEAN REVIVAL style home, designed by Phineas Paist in the 1930s, was brilliantly sited on the Coral Gables Waterway. It capitalizes on both the high elevation of the historic canal to the rear, and undulating low topography to the front. Landscape designer Robert Parsley has long consulted on this property.

The view from the street is of a deceptively flat lawn behind an extended band of white dwarf bougainvillea. A magnificent live oak tree, with an enormous hanging staghorn fern and orchid display, stands sentinel at the driveway entrance. Once through the gates, a palette of white, pale yellow and shades of green mirror the colors of the home. The wide front lawn dips down and undulates with the underlying natural coral rock formations of the Miami Rock Ridge, displaying the full façade of the home above.

A secluded coral rock pergola and adjacent coral-lined lily pond are reached via native limestone stairs that lead from the front door and driveway down into a secluded grotto. Aged overhead beams are so heavily covered with creeping fig (*Ficus pumila*) that the vine ceiling appears solid.

An arching bleeding heart vine (*Clerodendrum thomsoniae*) forms a gateway to the side and rear yards. A glass-enclosed cabana overlooking the canal is a space for casual entertaining and overnight guests. A cozy sitting terrace nearby is perfumed by gardenia and sheltered by large oak trees and a huge umbrella.

From this sitting area, several sets of Miami limestone steps lead down the terraced rock formations to a lower lawn and dock on the canal. The steps are lined with cascading agave growing among boulders. The lower lawn terrace houses a rustic table and benches carved from limestone and an outdoor fireplace tucked into the rock wall. From the dock and canal, bursts of color from red firecracker plants and blue plumbago brighten the exposed rock face, providing a scenic view for boaters on the canal. Protected red mangrove plants cling to the wall face and shoreline. Their submerged roots provide a sanctuary and nursery habitat to fish and crustaceans.

In a stark contrast to the more natural area of the lower lawn, clipped hedges surround a formal rose garden beyond the pool. This is an ambitious undertaking in a climate known for its heat and humidity.

Drawn to this historic waterside home and garden as soon as they first saw it, the owners feel it embodies the suburban tranquility of Coral Gables. They consider themselves to be caretakers for the next occupant, while enjoying their private slice of paradise.

LEFT *One of the pair of carved lions by the waterside steps.*

ABOVE *Street view with fig-covered columns and band of white bougainvillea beyond.*

RIGHT
A limestone-lined koi pond is tucked against a wall below the circular drive at the front of the home. Submerged pergola at left

BELOW LEFT
Tree-lined brick drive.

BELOW RIGHT
Limestone stairs leading from driveway to pergola and pond.

FACING BELOW LEFT
White water lilies (Nymphaea odorata) beside the trickling waterfall.

FACING BELOW RIGHT
Plants thrive in the craggy pockets of natural limestone. Burn jelly plant (Bulbine frutescens), at front, with white begonia, saw palmetto and foxtail fern (Asparagus densiflorus 'Myers').

TOP LEFT
Live oak (Quercus virginiana) *standing sentry at corner of wide front lawn, that dips down to follow the contours of the underlying rock.*

TOP RIGHT
A side yard archway with bleeding heart vine.

RIGHT
A small formal garden of fragrant tea and English roses can be glimpsed from the pool patio.

ABOVE *Agave, firecracker plant and wart fern (Microsorum scolopendrium) cascade down the rock face.*

BELOW *The pool terrace and benches offer front row viewing of the activity on the canal from the shade of a favorite oak. Crown of thorns plant (Euphorbia milii) at right.*

LEFT
Cascades of agave line the natural stone steps from the patio to the waterway.

ABOVE
Garden path to the canalside dock.

ABOVE *Large, dramatic remnants of the Miami Rock Ridge, with fireplace on lower lawn terrace.*

FACING TOP *Creeping fig cloaks the chimney of a fireplace built into the hillside.*

FACING BELOW *Stone table and benches offer access to the fireplace and views along the canal.*

FOLLOWING *Limestone banks of the Coral Gables waterway, with red mangrove* (Rhizophora mangle) *and plumbago* (Plumbago auriculata) *cascading to water's edge.*

PATHS TO SERENITY

L USH VEGETATION AND HIDDEN CORNERS with colorful potted plants surround a Mediterranean Revival home on a large lot in Pinecrest. Bubbling fountains and pools, antique statuary and sculptures as well as thoughtfully placed plant material, all reflect the owners' lifetime of collecting and sensitivity to the environment.

Several past owners and designers have influenced the design of this garden, along with Hurricane Andrew, which arrived in 1992. The damage to plant life from this Category 5 storm was substantial in this area of Miami-Dade County, but several royal palms and hardy live oaks survived. Shortly thereafter, a baobab tree was planted to further anchor this portion of the yard. Native primarily to Madagascar's dry deciduous forests, some species of baobab can reach heights of close to 100 feet and trunk diameters of 23 to 36 feet. Combined with beautiful live oaks, this glorious tree canopy has created a special habitat from which the inspiration for this garden evolved.

Densely planted understory foliage unites elements in a vast array of colors and textures. The home's current owners, along with horticulturist Frederick Hubbard, have enjoyed growing "nearly everything that can be grown," as long as it "sings to them personally." Likewise, historic and contemporary sculptures are also at home here. An extensive collection of Buddhist statues and Asian-inspired sculptures and urns blends

in naturally with the jungle-like setting. An extensive collection of bromeliads and blooming vines punches through the palette of green and provides year-round color.

Formally arranged arched entries and windows lead from the arrival court through the house to the swimming pool, and on to the raised outdoor pavilion and reflecting pool along the central axis. The formality ends there, as dense and varied plant material starts to shape the garden. Visitors are then treated to a delightful journey through a series of garden rooms.

In a grove of tall palms, three Buddhist musician statues appear to play along with sounds from a nearby

waterfall and pond. A cluster of tiny houses sits among moss and ferns in an elevated garden. Terraced reflecting basins are home to fish and water lilies. Prized jabuticaba, or Brazilian grape trees, flank the view to the reflecting pond, the fruits of which are enjoyed by the owners, raccoons and squirrels alike.

Bucking the stereotypical suburban penchant for tennis courts and open grass lawns, this family created a backyard habitat that embraces the natural world, and enriched it with large canopy trees, plants and water. Their hope is that others will also be so inspired to start planting for the future.

LEFT *Carved sandstone sculpture with potted orchids.*

ABOVE *Serene view from the pool cabana overlooking formal lily pond.*

BELOW *Gold finger plant* (Juanulloa aurantiaca), *at left. Potted fireball bromeliads* (Neoregelia 'Fireball'), *with Cyperus papyrus in pond.*

FACING TOP *Pink angel trumpet behind papyrus, gold finger at left.*

FACING MIDDLE *Caribbean heliconia* (Heliconia caribea) *as backdrop for terraced lily pond.*

FACING BOTTOM *Ground orchids atop carved pilaster.*

Shady sitting area beside grotto-like pond and waterfall.

MIDDLE
Trunks of teddy bear palm (Dypsis leptocheilos), at left. Bismarck palm (Bismarckia nobilis), at right.

BELOW
Pots of bromeliads and bougainvillea bring color to a primarily green landscape.

RIGHT
Trio of Buddhist musician sculptures at base of royal palms. Thai reullia (Ruellia elegans) in foreground.

FACING
BELOW RIGHT
Golden shrimp plant (Pachystachys lutea) gives constant color.

FACING
BELOW LEFT
Red leaves of croton (Codiaeum variegatum) with deep green lady palm (Rhapis excelsa).

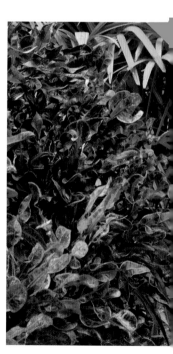

ABOVE LEFT *A variety of textures within a sea of green.*

LEFT *Giraffe sculptures beside a prized baobab tree.*

MODERNIST PRECISION

An INTERNATIONALLY RENOWNED art collector with a fine eye for design was a keen participant in every aspect of creating this lovely home and garden on Biscayne Bay. The owner wanted to soften the home's strong modern geometry and be surrounded by greenery and water. The garden blurs the stark horizontal and vertical lines of the home, creating a canvas for displaying art within the landscape. A subtle palette of white, grey, silver and green allows the art to shine.

Care and ingenuity were needed by Savino & Miller Design Studio to create a garden that is both intimate and grand. The entrance sequence from street to bay is a seamless experience, allowing the property to feel much larger through repetition of simple materials. Water is a central theme that weaves the garden areas together, appearing to flow from the bay to the courtyard and back, beginning with the meandering rill that originates at the street side gate

A grove of silver buttonwood trees provides privacy and billowy softness to the street façade, while just inside the wall, the sculptural branches form a secluded allée guiding visitors through a magical space filled with art, trickling water and lush beds of fern. A striking silk floss tree lends structure and color. Rather than dominating the small lot, two separate driveways are made integral to the garden as flowing green courtyards.

A tranquil three-story atrium and water garden in the heart of the property mark the transition from street side to bay side, and from outside to inside. Water tumbles from the wall amidst a clever slot garden filled with air plants and orchids. An outdoor dining and lounge area below the home blurs the line between bay and street, through the central atrium.

The infinity edge pool is perfectly placed to reflect the sky and bay, and its surrounding water rills enhance the impression of water flowing uninterrupted through the garden. The pool garden is designed for both solitary lounging and entertaining seated parties of 100. From here, the owner enjoys watching the morning sunrise or the moon reflected in the water.

The garden includes hardy natives immune to the unforgiving salt and wind exposure, with tall bamboo and palms at ground level providing green curtains for upper living areas. Planters and pergolas built into balconies soften the home's façade, while curtains of papyrus offer privacy, and jasmine lends fragrance.

The highly choreographed entry sequence is re-markable for such a small property. There is a sense of discovery as one passes through the simple gateway into a modern version of a woodland with trickling stream, on toward the atrium, and out through doors to the expanse of the bay.

In this modern garden, there is a feeling of superb balance and counterpoint. It is spa-like and modern, yet relaxed. The landscape is detailed, though not over-whelmed by the grandeur of the setting.

LEFT *Courtyard and sculpture in the evening.*

ABOVE *Horizontal bands of subtle gray and green materials add layers of interest and privacy from the street.*

TOP
Alternating bands of porous pavement serve as driveway and courtyard.

MIDDLE
Highly textured beds of Boston fern

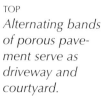

BELOW
Front gate entrance, at right, leads to internal courtyard and a bosquet of beautiful silver buttonwood trees, native to Florida.

FACING TOP
Rough bark of buttonwood is perfect for hanging orchids. A screw pine (Pandanus utilis) *on stilt-like prop roots at corner.*

FACING BELOW
The unusual thorny trunk of the silk-floss (Ceiba speciosa), *at rear.*

FACING ABOVE *Evening in front court.*

FACING BELOW *Night view of internal entry atrium. The pond holds containers of the truly tropical red ceiling wax palm* (Cyrtostachys renda), *and peace lily* (Spathiphyllum spp.).

ABOVE *Simple lawn panels surrounded by decking extend the entertainment area.*

BELOW *Deck with lighting integrated into bench. These native plants and coconuts tolerate salt conditions.*

Restoring a
Pine Rockland

An extraordinary transformation in Miami's Wynwood neighborhood has turned a once barren city lot into a thriving pine rockland, and an inspirational model for environmental preservation.

When purchased in 2007, the property contained a home and two trees and a patch of scrubby lawn. When helping plant a palm on a nearby property, the owner, a leading patron of artists and local institutions, including Fairchild Tropical Botanic Garden, learned of the underlying Miami Rock Ridge formations running through this neighborhood. Knowing that pine rocklands are globally imperiled ecosystems found only in Miami-Dade County, the Florida Keys and portions of the Bahamas, he was inspired to uncover the true rockland beneath his barren lot as an experimental restoration and demonstration site.

With the assistance of several local organizations that promote protection and restoration of these ecosystems, including Fairchild's Connect to Protect Network and the Institute for Regional Conservation (IRC), the owner researched the plants that could be grown in a rockland. Limestone outcroppings typically support a canopy of Florida slash pine and sabal palms, with a loose and airy herbaceous understory. The owner removed more than two feet of soil and rubble that filled several old solution holes which are now exposed. He used the rubble and soil to make retaining walls and raised areas that enhance the new topography.

With expert advice, appropriate plant material was purchased and installed. The owner arranged grasses, vines, palms, trees and shrubs in natural groupings along a gravel path resembling an "Iowa farm road" that reminded the owner of his Midwest origins. Plants are labeled for easy identification. This sandy track rises and dips as it traverses the length of the property, now passing four natural solution holes. The native plants dispersed throughout the double lot create strolling paths and shady sitting areas, where the air is cool and the light is filtered. The result is an enchanting, completely natural environment where birds, bees and butterflies frequent the many rare, endangered and

threatened plants. Light shines through the red trumpet blossoms of man-in-the-ground vine as it scrambles over large clumps of coontie, catching the eye like stained glass. Fragrances of Simpson's stopper and locustberry waft through the garden, and almost two dozen planted Florida slash pines make steady progress, thriving in their natural environment.

LEFT *Silver thatch palm with coontie and gamagrass in foreground.*

ABOVE *West Indian lilac* (Tetrazygia bicolor), *with showy white and yellow flower clusters in foreground, is listed as threatened by the state of Florida. Slash pine was formerly one of the dominant trees within the Miami-Dade County landscape.*

FACING TOP *Silver saw palmetto in foreground, with sabal palmetto beyond the sandy track. Limestone rubble fill excavated from the natural solution holes is used in retaining walls.*

FACING BELOW *Where once there was only hardscrabble lawn, sabal palms and slash pine offer shade to a meandering sandy drive.*

TOP *Native plants scramble above and below retaining walls in casual harmony. Pineland croton* (Croton linearis) *at left foreground, with Elliott's love grass* (Eragrostis elliottii) *in middle of drive.*

ABOVE *Coontie* (Zamia integerifolia, *often shown as* Z.pumila) *at left, West Indian lilac at right, with American beautyberry* (Callicarpa americana) *in foreground.*

OPPOSITE, CLOCKWISE FROM TOP LEFT

1 *New 'candle' growth of slash pine.*

2 *Pineland croton (left) and rougeplant* (Rivina humilis) *(right).*

3 *Coral hoarypea* (Tephrosia angustissima var. corallicola rosia) *is endangered in Florida.*

4 *Pineland heliotrope* (Heliotropium polyphyllum) *naturally occurs in moist pinelands and coastal areas.*

5 *Endangered man-in-the-ground* (Ipomoea microdactyla) *vine scrambles over a coontie.*

6 *Swallowtail butterfly resting on an American beautyberry.*

A Modernist Retreat

THE OWNERS OF THIS MODERNIST GEM, who might well prefer living in a tree house, asked landscape architect Raymond Jungles to assist them in renovating an uninspired 1957 house which was located on an island dredged from Biscayne Bay in 1924 by pioneering Miami Beach developer Carl Fisher. They wanted their interiors to seamlessly meld with the outdoors, and their views to be directed toward the garden. They requested seating areas that would incorporate their collection of Brazilian furniture, and an environment that would encourage quiet contemplation.

The property's most notable architectural intervention is introduced in the entry garden, which lies between two auto courts. A pergola, floating concrete steps, aquatic sculpture garden, and pivoting front door welcome visitors. As the door opens, interior and exterior elements fuse, and long views both through the house and out into the garden are revealed. The exterior materials are used on the house's ground plane, walls, and ceiling, further linking the spaces.

Long walls of windows connect the primary exterior spaces with the interior, allowing in both views and light. Corner windows magnify these opportunities; the glazing is frosted above exterior equipment areas where no view is desired. A favorite garden room with modern louvers was expanded so that it opens to the surrounding private courtyard garden. An outdoor dining area with a built-in table and cooktop was created adjacent to the kitchen, to encourage a union with nature.

To create privacy, the landscape architects chose indigenous gumbo limbo to provide the primary tree canopy with Jamaican caper, marlberry, silver saw palmetto, golden creeper, and coontie to accent the understory layer. The landscape is further dotted with numerous palms of varying heights and interest features.

The scale of the swimming pool was reduced to make room for a wet deck and alternate patio, perfect for lounging. The owners now have many uses for this newly designed area, and also have a long view across the garden to classic royal palms whose fronds wave against the skyline.

LEFT *Pavilion patio.*

ABOVE AND FOLLOWING *Front entrtance combines an aesthetic mix of low maintenence palms and bromeliads surrounding a lily pond and sculpture.*

ABOVE *Clustering rhaphis and bamboo-like cabada palms frame the view to the second-floor lanai.*

BELOW *View from the open air second-floor lanai.*

FACING TOP TO BOTTOM *The outdoor dining area, the pavilion and the pool form a harmonious outdoor room for entertaining, and extend the living spaces into the garden.*

ABOVE *The pavilion is the centerpiece of the back garden, framed by a combination of hardy native trees.*

RIGHT *The architecture perfectly integrates the living room, the pavilion and the pool.*

INSPIRED BY THE ORIENT

I N SOUTH FLORIDA, where so much appears recently arrived, enduring connections to the land do exist. Deep
in southwestern Miami-Dade County, four generations
of plant lovers deeply extended their roots into the rocky
soil of this remarkable property. Through their efforts,
what was once a turkey farm has been transformed over
the years into a tropical paradise of orchids and art.

The current owner is a renowned plantsman who
began collecting orchids when he was 10. Once dev-
astated by Hurricane Andrew, the property is now filled
with thousands of orchids and exotic plants in countless
colors and forms that grow from the ground up to the
tree canopies.

"After Andrew, there wasn't a green leaf anywhere
on the property," he notes. "The giant *Bischofia javani-
ca*, which my grandfather planted about 80 years ago,
was severely damaged. We righted as many of the top-
pled trees as we could, trimmed the damaged trees and
hoped for the best."

The giant, ancient-looking trees have become part
of a wonderland dotted with gazebos, chickee huts,
ponds and enclosures for colorful birds.

While traveling, the lush tropical gardens of Asia especially appealed to the owner who has recreated them
in his own paradise. Asian art is displayed throughout
the garden and is at home amid the jungle-like setting,
adorned with some of the world's most exotic orchids.

A 100-foot long pergola supports a magnificent display of Indian clock vine and rare green jade
vine. An old solution hole was further excavated
and was turned into a freshwater pool that is now
home to myriad fish as well as a resident alligator.
Decks and bridges were added over the course of years,
along with a gentle waterfall.

This breathtaking garden is what the owner describes as "a work-in-progress, and a work of love, for
more than 30 years." It is a special haven for wildlife
and "a place of beauty and serenity."

LEFT *Magnificent spray of* Schombodiacrium orchidglade *orchid, a cross of* Schomburgkia undulata *and* Diacrium bicornutum.

ABOVE *A serene, temple-like space with angel-wing begonia, shell ginger and vandaceous orchids accenting a Buddha fountain from Thailand.*

FACING *A cigar-form orchid* (Schomburg-kia tibicinis) *mounted above mounds of bromeliads and pink kalanchoe. The large gumbo limbo* (Bursera simaruba) *in background is one of the survivors of Hurricane Andrew.*

TOP *Font entrance with variegated Song of India* (Dracaena reflexa) *and pink begonias.*

MIDDLE LEFT *Vanda orchids.*

MIDDLE RIGHT *A Cuban petticoat palm* (Copernicia macro-glossa), *with persistent older leaves just beginning to form its characteristic "petticoat".*

ABOVE *A musical Buddha among aloe and Song of India.*

FACING *Pergola with Indian clock vine* (Thunbergia mysorensis) *and green jade vine* (Strongylodon macrobotrys).

ABOVE *An orange* Epidendrum radicans *orchid next to a cast bronze tortoise from Thailand.*

RIGHT *Hanging clusters of jade vine and potted orchids.*

BELOW *View toward the deck and the solution hole, now teeming with life.*

FOLLOWING *The excavated solution hole is now surrounded by waterfalls, ferns and orchids.*

FACING TOP *A restful place beneath the orchids* (Schombodiacrium orchidglade).

FACING BELOW *Rescued exotic birds are at home here in this tropical environment.*

ABOVE *Kuan Yin, Goddess of Mercy sculpture with offering of blossoms from Morning Song 'Crownfox' orchid.*

FLORIDA PRIMORDIAL

For this South Dade homeowner, the devastation of Hurricane Andrew in 1992 ultimately turned into inspiration that resulted in this property's reinvention from a mango grove to a cypress swamp bursting with life.

The transformation included acquiring a neighboring property and substantially expanding an existing pond to a more natural shape. Then came the addition of topography, islands, bridges and waterfalls. The real magic occurred with the addition of cypress trees, and an abundance of plants native to the Big Cypress National Preserve and Everglades National Park. A parade of wildlife and plants has independently arrived on the scene, and where there was once barren lawn, an extraordinary ecosystem now exists.

"This garden is such an expression of who I am: someone who loves the outdoors," offers the owner. "I planted natives where they like to go, but a lot of them just came in on their own, and I allowed them to stay. The native plants have been so happy to take over that there isn't much maintenance, except for thinning so we can enjoy the flora. It's turned out to be as easy as any other yard."

In addition to bald cypress, the upper canopy layer of this garden has been formed with native trees such as gumbo limbo and slash pine. Other habitat anchors include native palms, pond apple and an assortment of flowering natives. The pond holds tarpon, bass, snook, bream and gar, with mosquito fish that keep the traditional pests to a manageable level.

The homestead's vast native plant collection was assembled through many years of swapping with friends and acquisitions from the Native Plant Society. The owner is particularly proud of his buttonwood and red and black mangrove specimens. Native orchids cling to the cypress, and an artificial alligator tucked among the sawgrass is cause for a double take.

Trees and limestone lining the waterfall and water channels are cloaked in tiny ferns and begonias, and clusters of cypress knees at the base of giant trees add a feeling of fantasy to this remarkable garden.

Rustic benches made of found wood offer picturesque options for resting along the pond edge.

"A friend taught me the Everglades back country, and now I know it like the back of my hand. I used to wonder how the Everglades wilderness could be right in the city's backyard," notes the owner. "Now, I have a little wilderness in my own backyard."

LEFT *The 'knees' of bald cypress trees (Taxodium distichum) huddled at pond edge.*

ABOVE *Spanning the pond is a rustic boardwalk with built-in seat and fish-feeding perch.*

ABOVE
*Delicate leaves of the bald cypress tree contrast with the sturdy leaves of the swamp-dwelling native, giant leather fern (*Acrostichum danaeifolium*).*

LEFT
Bald cypress trunks form buttresses with age. A large gumbo limbo tree is seen in the distance.

RIGHT
The calm pool reflects the sky, casting dappled light onto the undersides of leaves.

TOP *A small central island hosts native sabal palms and a red mangrove* (Rhizophora mangle).

ABOVE *Through the dense foliage, a raised waterfall can be glimpsed in the distance.*

RIGHT *The massive concrete-like trunk of a 'volunteer' royal palm* (Roystonea regia) *is seen beyond the many native sat-inleaf trees* (Chrysophyllum oliviforme) *along the woodland walk. Native yellow pineland lantana* (Lantana depressa), *at right.*

A Coral Gables Jewel

Every square inch of the yard surrounding this 1926 Mediterranean Revival home in Coral Gables has been used to create a tableau of plants and distinctive objects. The owner's decades-long devotion to garden tours and botanical gardens led to the selection of many plants for their unique variegation or texture, such as a collection of epiphytic ferns, with long, flat patterned fronds resembling crocodile hide. A large pergola covered by fuchsia bougainvillea provides shade and support for myriad carefully collected orchids and bromeliads. A succession of fragrant, flowering plants includes tea olives, gardenias and orchids.

The garage and home's external walls and dense plantings along its rear boundary create a private courtyard that is a true outdoor living room. Collections of potted plants include both rare and common specimens of varying colors, textures and sizes that are often rearranged in order to highlight peak beauty. Favorites include the highly unusual Joey palm, which occupies a prominent pot near a water feature. This trunkless palm, endemic to the rainforest slopes and ridge tops of Southeast Asia, has large spectacular leaves, growing directly from underground rootstock. Other exceptional palms that enhance the view through the pergola include a beautifully nurtured Cuban old man palm, a licuala palm from the South Pacific, and *Arenga undulatifolia* from Southeast Asia.

Many of the plants were acquired from Fairchild Tropical Botanic Garden member plant sales and specialized local growers. The home's small yard allows for a high level of ongoing personal involvement in a space its owners describe as "a variegated hodgepodge of loved things we just can't live without." It is also a noteworthy example of how a true specimen garden can be created in a very small area.

ABOVE *Potted plants are easily arranged to enhance the outdoor living room.*

RIGHT *Potted imperial bromeliad* (Alcantarea imperialis), *and strap-leaved crocodile fern* (Microsorum musifolium 'Crocodyllus'), *anchor the pergola columns beneath a mass of brilliantly-colored bougainvillea.*

ABOVE *The outdoor living room.*

BELOW *Orchids and bright red stalk of the sealing wax palm*
(Cyrtostachys renda) *on right .*

RIGHT *Beyond the pergola, a collection of favorite palms form a green privacy
wall. Ruffled fronds of the* Arenga undulatifolia *from SE Asia (left), ruffled fan
palm* (Licuala grandis) *from Vanuatu (center) and a Cuban old man palm*
(Coccothrinax crinita) *on the right.*

BELOW *The richly textured garden features the fibrous trunk of an old man palm, broad strap-leaves of imperial bromeliad, narrow-leaved silver bromeliad* (Alcantarea odorata), *and dark green tufts of mondo grass* (Ophiopogon japonicus). *The old man palm is a rare species from Cuba, and is a favorite among palm collectors.*

FACING ABOVE *A Buddha rests next to a rare* Itaya amicorum *palm, native to lowland rainforests in the western Amazon basin.*

FACING BELOW *Clustered blue pots at the base of the bougainvillea include a variegated lady palm* (Rhapis excelsa).

LAKESIDE HIDEAWAY

THE FIRST VIEW THROUGH this tree-studded Coral Gables property is down to a secluded marshy shoreline. Architect Suzanne Martinson thoughtfully slipped the home and driveway into an existing hardwood hammock landscape without disturbing any mature trees during the home's construction. Landscape architect Deena Bell Llewellyn assisted the owners with the landscape design.

The property's thick canopy is composed largely of native trees. Orchids tucked into large oaks introduce splashes of color. Clustered beds of native saw palmetto, tropical begonias and delightful ornamentals such as giant leopard plants define edges.

The home's wide porches, metal roof, wood siding and local limestone recall a Florida cracker-style aesthetic favored by pioneers who settled in South Florida.

The driveway is constructed of local limestone set in sand and arranged around existing live oaks that allow water to flow freely to the trees and provide room for roots to grow. An interrupted limestone curb and gravel band at the low edge of the drive manage rain runoff.

A swimming pool area on the sloping lawn incorporates the use of limestone in the retaining walls, seat wall caps and pool deck. An infinity edge with waterfall was created where the lawn meets the lake. In addition to providing an elegant contrast to the stone pool deck, the black tiled pool interior reflects the sky and nearby trees. The lake's reflection of the sky and surrounding marsh grasses, gives it the appearance of extending directly into the lawn.

A cabana and a fire pit are located across from the pool, accented with a variety of comfortable outdoor furniture, including pastel-colored Adirondack chairs. As the lawn slopes down toward the edge of the lake, broad grassy terraces and limestone stairs provide ease of access on the steeper slope. The open lawn between these sitting areas and the pool creates a much-used multi-purpose entertainment area. The landscape in these areas has been kept to a minimum in order to maximize the expansive view of the lake. Hanging basket chairs on the deck are an ideal place to sit and watch children on a zip line and view the sunset.

LEFT *The infinity edge pool appears to merge with the lake beyond.*

ABOVE *Local limestone pavers set in sand surround the preserved oaks, creating ample room for cars or entertaining.*

TOP *The existing tropical hardwood hammock was carefully preserved, with only a gateway for access.*

ABOVE *Low beds of saw palmetto and giant leopard plant (Farfugium japonicum 'Giganteum') create a simple green edge for the wrap-around porch.*

TOP *Cozy sitting areas flank the open lawn.*

ABOVE *The seat wall, patio and infinity edge pool step gracefully down the slope.*

FOLLOWING *View from cabana to the lake.*

MAJESTY ON THE BAY

Arare and dramatic Coral Gables promontory provides an exceptional setting for enjoying Biscayne Bay and a waterfront lifestyle. The owners desired a romantic, yet family-friendly setting for a new home, designed to look like it had been there for a century. The owners and landscape designer, Santi Diaz, wanted large, mature trees to give this property its feel of a long-ago established landscape. They had massive specimens that set records for their size, painstakingly barged to this building site.

A strangler fig, weighing 140 tons at the time of its move, occupies the property's highest point, and appears to stand guard over the entire estate. A remarkable African baobab specimen with an enormous gnarled root system, reportedly brought from Tanzania as a sapling in 1908 and carefully nurtured elsewhere, has now found its permanent home at the front gateway. The base often resembles an elephant's foot.

The rear lawn is graced with the magnificent canopy of a maturing *Ceiba pentandra*. This specimen came from Cuba during the Mariel boatlift of 1980. Ceiba is a genus of very large deciduous trees found in the Caribbean and Central and South America, reaching upwards

of 200 feet, and is the tallest of trees in the Amazon rainforest. Many cultures regard these trees as sacred or symbolic. One of the many, but most recognized, common names for this tree is kapok.

The entire landscape has been treated with meticulous care. A loggia off the breakfast room offers panoramic views eastward over the pool to Biscayne Bay and along the southern point of the promontory. Dining and lounging terraces tucked into gardens step down from the home toward the water. A mid-level terrace is an ideal location for welcoming each new sunrise.

Along the water's edge, a series of private seating areas and niches for sculpture display have been tucked into the gardens.

An open cabana was sited atop a ridge to catch bay breezes and wide views over an expansive lawn and sandy coconut grove. Billowy grasses and colorful bird-of-paradise slope down to the water's edge where curving stairs step directly into the bay.

Most notable is the great care that was taken to ensure that each enormous specimen was given ample room to develop, unimpeded to full maturity.

LEFT *A large strangler fig* (Ficus aurea) *guards the home's bayside entrance.*

ABOVE *A massive African baobab has adapted well to its new Miami home, becoming one with the wall.*

ABOVE *Golden bamboo brightens the length of the entry drive.*

ABOVE *Two-tier koi pond in the center of the motor court.*

BELOW *The front entrance is cloaked in bougainvillea and the woody, evergreen creeping fig* (Ficus pumila).

LEFT *The strangler fig dominates the bayside lawn.*

TOP *Landscaped beds frame views of the bay and the family's sculpture collection.*

ABOVE *View toward house from the pool.*

ABOVE *View toward open cabana. Broad beds of grasses and bird-of-paradise* (Strelitzia reginae) *stabilize steep slopes.*

TOP *Terraces and steps descend into Biscayne Bay beside a sculpture of children playing.*

BELOW *Bayside coconut palm grove.*

FOLLOWING *Miami's skyline with illuminated coconut palms and sculpture in the foreground.*

OASIS IN THE GROVE

"I WANTED TO CREATE my own little world, a hiding place, and it just keeps evolving," says the owner of this tiny garden. "It is a hidden treasure; so unexpected. Everything seems to grow here. There is so much life — honey bees in the wall, peacocks, parrots, raccoons and foxes. It's all about energy, and yet, there is such a sense of serenity."

Originally intended to be a property purchased for rehab and resale, the garden that grew from a once barren lot is now a celebration of all living things.

Home and garden flow smoothly together through windows and doors, and the elevated patio, once envisioned as an enclosed room, has been left open to fully embrace the elements. The patio is defined by a railing that is an artful re-creation of arching red mangrove roots. Antique torch lamps and textured columns with vines add life and character to this inviting sitting area. Whimsical sculptures and colorful tiles brighten nooks and crannies of this small garden, and the sound of the waterfall fills the enchanting space.

The narrow green canyon formed by the patio and a tall, vine-covered rear wall acts as a greenhouse to shelter the most delicate plants, creating a tiny wonderland for orchids of all kinds. Orchids are clearly a favorite of the owner who has them on display throughout this playful and colorful garden. Within this grotto-like place resides a stone Buddha that gazes toward a secluded bench, a favorite place for contemplation.

One side of the front door is flanked by a striking wall of native coral rock mixed with pink granite, black lava, and a sprinkling of crystals and gemstones. The composition is imbued with communal treasures lovingly placed to create a work of art, an opportunity for shared memories with friends. The wall is the largest of three such panels, a meaningful repetition throughout the home and garden. Coral and crystals form walls and vignettes in many corners of the garden, where the act of arranging and rearranging each composition is soothing to the soul.

LEFT *Fanciful gate created by neighbor and copper artist, Jim Lewk, marks the entrance to an enchanted back yard.*

ABOVE *Massive pots of bromeliads frame the entrance. Three royal palms (Roystonea regia) are the first expression of the owner's significant number of palms.*

TOP *Low bedding plants beneath tall palms leave the middle view open, adding dimension to the front yard.*

RIGHT *A welcoming wall beside the front door is composed of native coral, limestone, granite, and crystals, shared by friends and placed to channel energy.*

FACING *The Old Chicago brick walkway is lined with a colorful and highly textured palette of bromeliads, crotons and foxtail fern (Asparagus densiflorus 'Myers').*

TOP LEFT *Red ginger* (Alpinia purpurata) *beside antique torch lights and copper leaves on the porch's mangrove railing.*

TOP MIDDLE *Ti plant* (Cordyline fruticosa) *gives a bright pop of color, even when orchids are not in bloom.*

TOP RIGHT *Beautiful texture and color combinations with bromeliad, asparagus fern and anthurium.*

BELOW LEFT *A Vanuatu fan palm* (Licuala grandis) *against a vine-cloaked rear wall.*

BELOW MIDDLE *Dracaena offer dense greenery in a narrow space.*

BELOW RIGHT *A vast collection of blooming orchids, many of which were discarded by others.*

FACING *The rear porch is made extraordinary by Jim Lewk's sculptural railings in copper that mimic red mangrove roots, branches and leaves twining up the columns.*

LEFT
Close-up of mangrove root railing copper sculpture.

BELOW
Casual seating on porch, over-looking pool.

FACING TOP
View from narrow path below porch toward pool.

FACING MIDDLE
Art tiles beneath waterfall.

FACING BELOW
Pool with waterfall topped with mounded bromeliads. Vandaceous orchids in foreground.

BAYFRONT VISTAS

CHOSEN FOR ITS PRIVACY AND VIEWS of downtown Miami, Coconut Grove and Key Biscayne, this waterfront property is located on a peninsula overlooking Biscayne Bay. When purchased in the early 1990s, the garden included a modern pool and fountain elements in a lush, but somewhat overgrown setting. The new owners desired a classical architectural style and requested that landscape architect Deena Bell Llewellyn create a more open and elegantly restrained landscape to serve the family's recreation needs and accommodate large philanthropic events.

Upon acquiring an empty lot next door, the home was seamlessly expanded. A complete transformation of the landscape included the construction of a new guesthouse and garage, with a soothing color palette of pale yellow, blue and purple uniting the structures. Mature trees were shifted to the property's side edges, creating instant privacy and opening vistas across the expansive yard and out to the bay. The pool and fountain basins were reshaped with classically inspired forms and tile patterns.

In keeping with the family's love of fitness and the outdoors, a series of garden rooms was designed for living and entertaining in the open air, along with a large outdoor kitchen and poolside lounge. The wide water-

front garden includes an elegant fountain basin, whose formality is relieved with whimsical frog sculptures preserved from the original design.

The garden extends along the seawall, preserving views and breezes throughout the grounds. Broad sweeps of lushly planted beds in favorite colors create a soothing ambiance. Curtains of Spanish moss and bursts of colorful orchids glow in the sunshine.

The centerpiece of the motor court is an antique bronze sculpture and fountain basin. A nearby folly, originally surrounded by an herb garden, was turned into a yoga pavilion that appears to float above a koi pond within a tranquil Asian-inspired woodland. Pavilion walls were trimmed, and the roof was refined into a delicate bronze tracery that celebrates the original form

while embracing the natural elements. A tropical beach tucked within a grove of palm trees offers a perfect contrast to the more formal areas.

"We have the most amazing views," claim the owners, "including the ability to watch the fireworks of three different cities across the bay. We love being outdoors on the water, fishing, relaxing or exercising in the open air. The yoga pavilion is one of our favorite places of all." The owners have relayed, "It does not feel like a typical Florida landscape. It transports you to someplace else."

LEFT *View across pool to skyline of Miami.*

ABOVE *Broad planting beds anchor the shoreline, while framing views and offering privacy to the home's upper levels.*

ABOVE LEFT *Spanish moss* (Tillandsia usneoides) *and scores of orchids cloak the trees.*

LEFT *Driveway along front of home lined with palms and trees with orchids.*

ABOVE *Curtains of Spanish moss along the front driveway catch the afternoon sun.*

BELOW *Dramatic lighting of the jewel-like yoga pavilion and koi pond creates a magical space visible from the motor court and water.*

RIGHT ABOVE *Zen garden with granite bench beside yoga pavilion and koi pond.*

RIGHT BELOW *Dark green coontie (at left) and variegated dwarf schefflera (Schefflera arboricola 'Trinette') with red ginger lining path.*

ABOVE *A grove of coconut palms creates a lounging area framed by variegated dwarf schefflera and the prop roots of screw pine* (Pandanus utilis) *in foreground.*

RIGHT *Fire pit in coconut grove, with palm-like screw pine along water.*

FOLLOWING *Festive lighting of pool terrace with long view toward entertainment lawn and Miami. Stately Bismarck palm* (Bismarckia nobilis) *in foreground.*

FORMAL ELEGANCE

THIS ELEGANT PALLADIAN-STYLE HOME in Coral Gables is set within formal gardens, creating an ideal spot for viewing the bay and entertaining family. A dense hedge of ficus trees more than 40-feet tall forms an arching gateway. Beyond, a low wall and layers of vegetation create a surprising sense of welcome and serenity.

A formal garden, reminiscent of a French parterre, features twin curving pergolas, covered with purple queen's wreath vine. A round fountain basin backed by graceful iron gates creates a focal point from the home's upper windows. Clipped topiaries and shrubs provide structure for the garden, while magnificent specimens of South African *Encephalartos ferox* or Zululand cycads offer striking contrast with their vase-like form and "ferocious" spiny leaflets. Clipped bougainvillea and orchid displays add splashes of color to the queen's wreath in this largely green garden.

The formal garden is encircled by a driveway of hand-made bricks, ornamented with a pebble mosaic of mortared river stones. The carpet-like mosaic treatment is repeated on the pool terrace, contrasting with the limestone surfaces of the home's central atrium and pool surround.

Visitors enter a two-story Roman-style central atrium garden through grand columns. The area is accented with Macarthur palms, river stones, and a fountain. Stairs lead to the main entrance on the second floor loggia, where upon entering the home, the dramatic view of Biscayne Bay is revealed.

On the bay side, the garden remains true to its formal theme with uncluttered lawn panels, hedges, and topiary. The elegant pool is surrounded by twin jardinières of vibrant bougainvillea and pebble mosaics. The simple palette of green lawn and shrubs with the blue pool in the foreground allows the bay to be the central, magnificent experience of the second floor balcony. This home and garden effortlessly blend European architectural styles with the native and tropical plants of Florida to create a serene secret garden.

LEFT *View through gate to parterre garden and grand entry.*

ABOVE *View through archway of clipped ficus hedge to low wall encircling parterre garden.*

179

FACING TOP *Pleached ficus hedge offers complete privacy for the home and gardens within.*

FACING MIDDLE *Daytime view through ficus archway.*

FACING BELOW *Fountain with view along main axis through central atrium to Biscayne Bay.*

FACING TOP *Pebble mosaic motor court between home and parterre garden.*

FACING BELOW *Cross axis view through curving pergolas at parterre garden.*

ABOVE AND RIGHT *Clipped hedges include bougainvillea. Pergola vines are purple queen's wreath* (Petrea volubilis).

BELOW LEFT *Potted and clipped standards of bougainvillea and Japanese blueberry tree* (Elaeocarpus decipiens) *add height to the parterre.*

BELOW RIGHT *Balcony overlooking the garden.*

TOP
The shady drive circles around the parterre garden.

MIDDLE
Pergola and driveway at evening.

BELOW
A variety of orchids to the left of the path leading to the rear gardens.

FACING TOP
A trio of pongam trees (Pongamia pinnata), at left, with garcinia topiary on the bayside lawn.

FACING BELOW
Potted bougainvillea in urns overlooking the pool and bay.

Mediterranean Echoes

THE DESIGN OF THIS MEDITERRANEAN-STYLE oasis in Miami Beach was inspired by the architecture and gardens of Moorish Spain, where home, courtyard and garden blend seamlessly, and decorative arts are integral to the architecture. The 1928 home is the embodiment of old Miami Beach and greets visitors with a gracious porte cochere flanked by spiral columns, colorful Arabic tiles, and oversized urns.

With only three large trees on site, including a large banyan and a West Indian mahogany that once held an owner's pet monkey, a landscape design team had free rein to design a garden that celebrated the home and its Miami Beach setting. Landscape architects Susan J. Hall and Deena Bell Llewellyn, with assistance from designer Lewis Aqui, created a vibrant and comfortable landscape that is now completely in tune with the historic residence. The garden plantings evoke a feeling of vintage South Florida, including colorful crotons, gingers, angel's trumpet, cycads and ferns. While virtually none of this plant material is native to South Florida, they have naturalized in this area for such a long time that it appears they have always belonged.

The premier garden space is the interior courtyard and pool area. The courtyard is flanked on three sides by a Mediterranean Revival loggia, complete with arches, spiral columns and colorful Moorish tiles. The centerpiece is a magnificent eight-sided fountain basin, whose tile patterns match those of the Alhambra, the 14th-century palace in Spain.

Sicilian sculptor and tile artist Sergio Furnari designed three new art tile pieces: a stunning mural on the bottom of the pool, a mural backsplash in the summer kitchen, and a sculptural bench ideally situated for watching sunsets across the pool.

The southern view from the central loggia is enhanced by giant philodendron leaves spilling into the pool, backed by a dense planting of fishtail palms that offer privacy and a glimpse of the barely restrained jungle beyond. The cabana-style summer kitchen sits below an apartment created for the original owner's chauffeur. From the summer kitchen, the eastern view across the pool and a small lawn panel terminates at the stunning tile bench, which is framed by the banyan, and backed by the filigree-topped wall.

The sound of the fountain permeates this tranquil landscape so in tune with the architecture of the home and tropical setting, blurring the boundaries between indoors and out.

TOP LEFT *Painted tile bench detail.*

TOP RIGHT *Original filigree cast concrete wall ornamentation and new stone parking area. Porte cochere is flanked by tall mast trees* (Polyalthia longifolia).

FOLLOWING *Recent additions of a sculptural tile bench and wall ornamentation at the former driveway entrance appear as though original to the historic home.*

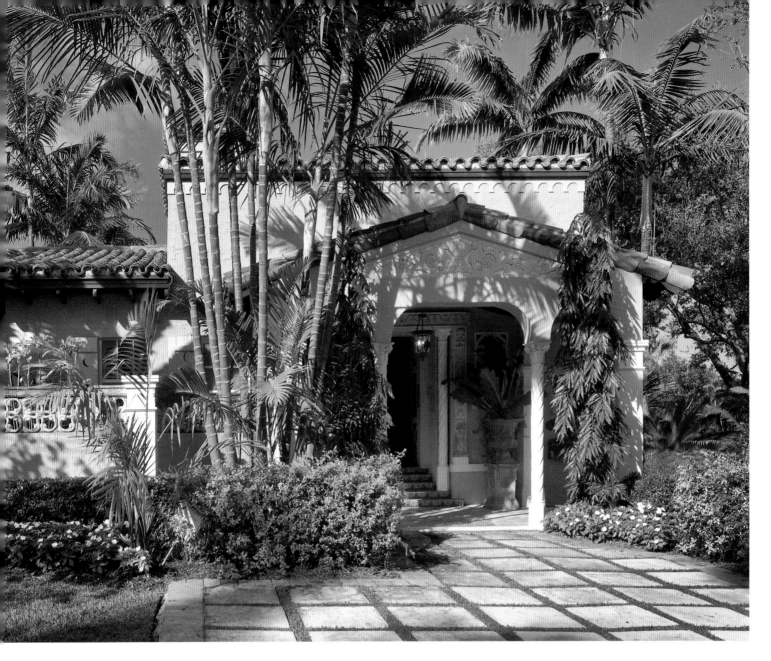

ABOVE LEFT *Porte cochere with oversized urns containing bird's nest anthurium. Cycad in foreground is a giant dioon (Dioon spinulosum).*

ABOVE RIGHT *Moorish tile and architectural details at front entrance served as inspiration for new and restored garden elements.*

FACING TOP *Internal court-yard, restored fountain, towering veitchia palms and columnar southern magnolia at loggia.*

FACING MIDDLE *Limestone bands and terracotta tiles with restored fountain.*

FACING BELOW LEFT *View from courtyard toward pool and summer kitchen cabana.*

FACING BELOW RIGHT *Crown of thorns and giant dioon accent original tiles and limestone.*

TOP *Fishtale palms and giant philodendron offer complete privacy.*

ABOVE *Pool with art tile details and narrow leafed croton.*

Celebrating Classicism

THE DESIRE FOR A UNIQUE personal sanctuary spurred the creation of a remarkable garden full of plants few would expect to survive in South Florida. Designer Jorge Sanchez employed tropical, subtropical and northern plants to capture the aesthetic of an English picturesque style landscape. Pleasing variety, irregularity, asymmetry, and interesting textures perfectly compliment the formality of the architecture.

"We really do enjoy sharing the garden with family and friends," say the owners. "We liked the idea of creating a property that is very different from the neighboring properties and from the typical tropical gardens in South Florida. We fell in love with the huge kapok tree, and it inspired us to have a collection of very large, very special trees."

The garden is designed to embrace an active young family, with elements that feed mind, body and soul. Within a series of romantic spaces, herbs, fruits and vegetables support a child's curiosity; a formal sunken garden doubles as a soccer stadium; and a charming playhouse folly occupies pride of place between the rose garden and the elegant pool terrace. Subtle labels identify the extraordinary collection of giant trees and specimens planted for beauty, fragrance and butterflies.

The garden journey begins with a drive through a formal allée of northern American sycamore trees toward the grand arrival court. Meandering pathways connect splendid garden rooms, guiding footsteps and rollerskates past ancient fountains and sculptures. Plants and features are placed to draw the eye and body from one garden to the next, providing a welcome departure from absolute symmetry.

A sense of mystery is woven throughout, with glimpses of the next charming space through gateways, around bends and beneath pleached hedges where playful passages have been carved. A dark crevice between rough-hewn boulders beckons the stroller to enter, where the reward is an enchanting grotto replete with candle niches and an echoing drip chamber.

A grand loggia anchors the primary view through the home across a sunken lily pond toward a raised mound crowned with a temple-like office. The southern façade of the home overlooks a formal sunken garden that hosts massive tent receptions as well as family soccer matches.

An elevated, highly manicured emerald green lawn of zoysiagrass forms the centerpiece of a large sun-dappled glade surrounded by enormous densely planted trees, creating a magical woodland perimeter. Fruit and citrus trees from the tropics reside with American elderberry shrubs and flowering azaleas from the north. A limestone path glows in moonlight to guide strollers through an extraordinary wonderland of billowy plants.

LEFT *View from Palladian-style motor court toward entrance gate.*

ABOVE *Inspired by the landscapes of New England, a magnificent allée composed of sycamore trees (Platanus occidentalis), also known as American planetree, lines a driveway of Belgian granite blocks.*

FACING TOP *Lily pond with angel trumpet trees* (Brugmansia spp). *and purple flowering giant potato trees* (Solanum macranthum) *behind.*

FACING MIDDLE *View from pool cabana toward elevated office.*

FACING BELOW *Colorful flowering begonias and sheltering live oak, one of the many large trees moved to the site.*

FACING TOP *Pool cabana designed for entertaining.*

FACING MIDDLE *West loggia and butterfly garden.*

FACING BELOW *View from west loggia.*

ABOVE
The playhouse folly and rose garden viewed from the children's vegetable garden.

RIGHT
The playhouse folly and butterfly garden viewed from the pool terrace.

FOLLOWING PAGES
The sunken garden hosts family soccer matches and large tent gatherings. Two huge sandbox trees (Hura crepitans), original to the property, tower over the garden.

FACING

CLOCKWISE FROM TOP LEFT

(1) *Baobab, the national tree of Madagascar.*

(2) Baobab tree at left, buttressed trunk of kapok in distance.

(3) *Crossandra lining the woodland walk.*

(4) *The prickled trunk of a sandbox tree, with tree bougainvillea and kapok in distance.*

(5) *View from woodland walk across the elevated lawn panel.*

(6) *A huge, buttressed red kapok tree (Ceiba pentandra) along the woodland walk, with tree-form bougainvillea in foreground.*

RIGHT
Interior of grotto with limestone walls and pebble mosaic floor.

BELOW LEFT
Orchid wall and bamboo behind cabana.

BELOW RIGHT
Mast tree (Polyalthea longifolia) forms a dense vertical screen behind antique Italian fountain basins.

FACING ABOVE
Woodland walk through stone archway of rock excavated on site.

FACING BELOW
Golden bamboo in sitting area behind elevated office.

FOLLOWING
View toward west loggia over lily pond. Pleached hedges of Eagleston holly separate the lovely garden rooms.

FORMALITY MEETS VERNACULAR

When purchased, this barren lot of compacted stone was the least desirable plot of land in a premier South Dade private waterfront community. What for years served as a surface parking lot was transformed into an elegant home site and garden with a refined Florida vernacular style.

Architect David Johnson and landscape architect Deena Bell Llewellyn created a gracious home with comfortable porches for enjoying bay breezes and garden views. Inspired by the old cracker-style architecture of South Florida, the large home was broken into smaller structures connected by glass-lined hallways, minimizing the overall impression of size. Broad porches with deeply overhanging roofs, and horizontal siding grounded by a coral rock foundation complete the effect. The hallways between the wings provide a clever opportunity to "bring the garden indoors" and are heavily planted with *Thrinax radiata*, or Florida thatch palms. These palms are native to the extreme southern mainland coast of Florida and points south, and have become endangered in the state of Florida. Hung with scores of colorful orchids, these palms grow well in high pH calcareous material, making them a perfect choice for this particular site. The courtyards that these palms anchor have crushed shells, coral and chunks of glass for mulch that glow and shimmer in the landscape lighting.

The home sits comfortably in its landscape, folded within low walls and sweeping beds of colorful groundcover plants. Welcoming front porches feature bay views, and large back porches are designed for entertaining, reading and enjoying the secluded pool area.

In order to integrate the pool more closely with the porch and summer kitchen that spans the rear of home, much of the rear lawn was raised and supported by large blocks of hatchet-formed, dry stack oolite stone. By offsetting two layers of oolite retaining walls, lower level plant beds were created, and the need for visually distracting railings was eliminated. Precast stairs and pavers in the lawn are made of tabby, a concrete created with lime, sand and oyster shells.

Melding French formal symmetry and native plant material, the elegant pool lawn is dominated by an

allée of royal palms. Crushed coquina rock paths border the raised lawn panel at the lowest level and an oolite fire pit with surrounding seat wall. The dense privacy plantings that surround this haven are a mixture of native shrubs and trees that take equally well to close trimming or leaving to nature. A sense of careful placement and quiet restraint is evident, and the overall impression is one of Old Florida, refined.

LEFT *Broad rear porch and path to the pool.*

ABOVE *The front of the home features a low wall and planting beds that preserve the view to Biscayne Bay.*

LEFT *View from the cabana sitting area toward the home.*

ABOVE *Cabana and lounging area.*

BELOW LEFT *Native royal palms frame the pool.*

BELOW RIGHT *A favorite view from the upper balcony shows the entire elevated pool terrace.*

TOP
A corner of the rear porch, overlooking the pool terrace sitting area.

MIDDLE
View from the lower pathway.

BELOW
Stair risers and retaining walls of oölitic limestone descend from the pool terrace toward surrounding gravel paths.

FACING TOP
Fire pit with seat wall.

FACING BELOW
A casual gravel path meanders around the pool terrace. Triangle palms, native to Madagascar, and a mixture of native shrubs, including silver buttonwood on the outer edges, are left natural.

A Personal Sanctuary

Since 1978, this South Miami garden has evolved under the abiding theme of a love of horticulture that nurtures and inspires, while offering therapy and solace. What began as a youthful interest in growing things became a career path that included work in a horticultural training program for disabled youth, ownership of an indoor tropical foliage business, and a love of "every kind of plant there is."

Along with professional evolution, this very personal garden has transitioned many times to accommodate a growing family, plants one could not live without, and plants abandoned by others. According to the owner, "The love of plants is more important than order, but I do aim for long term sustainability by putting the right plant in the right place. Where once there were only towering oaks, now," he proudly says, "I have my own little Fairchild."

After diagnosis of a progressive motor disorder, this committed gardener is adapting the landscape yet again to meet his abilities, deriving enormous satisfaction from both active and passive garden activities. With occasional assistance from family and volunteers, he shares this garden with others who have motor disabilities, offering therapy and the joy of communal gardening. An attractive assortment of raised beds furthers the ability to garden in spite of physical challenges and enhances the sense of independence.

Water gardens, mosaic tiles and a repetition of trellis and pottery elements form a binding narrative between garden rooms. Winding paths lead to hidden treasures and many shady resting spots along the way. Rare and common plants and cleverly repurposed materials spur cherished memories and stories throughout. Views from the home's interior and porches offer a multitude of colorful and engaging vistas.

The physical, emotional and temporal journey of the garden and gardeners has brought great reward and satisfaction. In this welcoming garden, there is room for creativity and acceptance, challenge and celebration.

FACING *Gateway with firespike* (Odontonema strictum), *a hummingbird magnet, at left.*

ABOVE *Gazebo, originally built for a garden wedding among the orchids and oaks.*

TOP *Artistic elements are tucked into the lush greenery.*

ABOVE *An imperial bromeliad* (Alcantarea imperialis) *dominates the plantings.*

ABOVE *Garden structures are created from a 'kit of parts', creating a rhythm that recurs through the garden.*

ABOVE LEFT *A telescope is a surprising find in the dense foliage.*

LEFT *Philodendron 'Rojo Congo' beneath a birdhouse.*

ABOVE *This Chinese fan palm is one of many 'volunteers' to find a permanent home here.*

FOLLOWING *Huge round leaves of begonia are a fine companion for delicate leaves of ferns, and the red powder puff shrub* (Calliandra haematocephalla). *The modern mosaic-tiled waterfall is part of a larger pond network.*

FACING ABOVE *A large ponytail palm* (Beaucarnea recurvata), *with swollen trunk, at left.*

FACING BELOW *Colorful mosaic tiles accent the outdoor bar.*

TOP *A collection of raised garden beds allow for standing or sitting while pursuing a favorite pastime.*

ABOVE *The woodland walk includes a favorite graceful bamboo* (Bambusa textilis gracilis).

TROPICAL COLORS

A LARGE ESTATE IN HOMESTEAD offers a series of painterly vignettes artfully arranged to create a multifaceted landscape for a couple that loves entertaining and the outdoors. The family's hobbies and long agricultural history in the area inspired them to paint their home in favorite tropical colors of papaya and purple.

Architect Charles Harrison Pawley designed the deep toned house. The garden was given early structure by the Avalon Gardens staff, who designed the extensive pond system and the driveway. Most recently, the team of horticulturist Debra DeMarco and landscape designer Carlos Somoza added the owners' favorite colors to the countless shades of tropical green. The designers incorporated each activity into the garden experience, specially timed for peak effect when the owners are in residence. Through clever use of seasonal plants, evolving tapestries of texture and color provide multiple views, and a delightful setting for the fancifully colored home.

Swaths of sprawling purple queen and perky *Plectranthus 'Mona Lavender'* are used as groundcover, and the subtle purple crown shafts of satake palms all combine to contrast and compliment the many sprays of orange throughout the garden. Even the koi in the formal fishponds match the color scheme. In this area, the river stones surrounding the limestone paths have been carefully laid to look like overlapping fish scales, creating a whimsical effect under one's feet.

The rear patio contains a free-form pool and pavilion, which are surrounded by large and lush planting beds. They contain a wide variety of both unusual and familiar plants, annuals and perennials that change with time and the season. Currently including more than 2,000 begonias, the focus of these beds is sweeping continuous color.

The stroll garden surrounding the home begins with a serene pond, waterfall and creek system, with delightful sitting areas, where the owners enjoy many evenings watching wildlife. Further along the stroll, an intimate white garden surrounding a small lawn provides a lovely afternoon sitting area.

A paved walkway and exercise trail weaves around the perimeter of this 10-acre estate, through groves of tropical ornamental and fruit trees, past a succulent garden featuring extraordinary plants from around the world, and finally to a jade vine-covered day pergola of limestone and wrought iron.

This garden of many lovely parts closely reflects the vision of its owners, allowing them to enjoy the outdoors surrounded by the vibrant colors they love.

ABOVE LEFT *Vibrant New Guinea impatiens allow the silver bromeliad* (Alcantarea odorata) *and a large cycad to shine.*

ABOVE *Dense tropical foliage is enlivened by bedding plants surrounding the colorful home. The purple crown shaft of the satake palm* (Satakentia liukiuensis) *is visible at center.*

ABOVE LEFT *Winding tree-lined entry drive.*

ABOVE RIGHT *The ornamental gate celebrates tropical fruit and vegetation.*

223

FACING *Large blocks of rustic limestone flank a side door.*

ABOVE *Broad swaths of purple queen* (Tradescantia pallida 'Purple Heart') *beneath triangle palm* (Dypsis decaryi).

BELOW *Impatiens drift toward elephant ears* (Colocasia esculenta 'Tea Cup') *at right.*

ABOVE *Tall bamboo and royal palm are anchored by bands of bedding plants.*

RIGHT ABOVE *Red button ginger (Costus woodsonii) and orange coleus add splashes of color.*

RIGHT BELOW *Rustic blocks of limestone lead past philodendron 'Burle Marx' and giant elephant ear (Colocasia gigantea).*

ABOVE *The African tulip tree (Spathodea campanulata) takes center stage among a collection of large specimens.*

RIGHT *The height of the banyan tree and bamboo attractively frame the distant palm, and the view to the interior gardens.*

A waterfall and lounging areas are tucked between the lush beds.

The outer edges of the pool deck are framed with vast beds of colorful annual and perennial plants.

The pool terrace is easily accessed from the home or a second floor balcony, from which the full garden tapestry can be appreciated.

Dense planting beds come right to the edges of the lagoon-style pool.

ABOVE *Up-lighting adds a sculptural quality to the ridged trunks of the palms.*

BELOW *A pool pavilion marks the transition to the open, park-like lawn.*

ABOVE *Lawn pathways lead through a palmetum to a tranquil pond.*

BELOW *Florida native horsetails* (Equisetum hyemale), *in the middle ground, provide a vertical contrast to bromeliads and sabal palms.*

ABOVE *View to the pond across mounds of begonias in the white garden.*

BELOW *The multilevel pond is a favorite resting place in the evenings.*

FOLLOWING *A large waterfall adds sound and motion to the peaceful setting.*

Low Country Charm

Between Biscayne Bay and the Snapper Creek canal, a tranquil home and garden combine a vision of a genteel South Carolina low country plantation with old Florida vernacular style.

The land for the custom home was chosen for its existing large live oak trees, and the house was carefully built within their sculptural canopies. One massive oak, deemed too precious to remove was carefully pruned to accommodate construction, and now grows through the deck and ceiling of the breezeway connecting the main house and garages.

The large Chicago brick patio provides a lovely space to entertain under the tall sheltering trees. A gently curving gravel driveway edged with the same brick adds subtle texture. Simple Old South ornamentation, collected by the owners, include such rustic elements as a massive molasses cauldron of the type traditionally used on sugar cane plantations. A wooded corner contains a brick fire pit encircled by rocking chairs.

The owners wanted their landscape designer Santi Diaz to focus on native plant material as much as possible, with very few flowering specimens interrupting the largely green palette. The existing oak and gumbo limbo trees provided anchors for the design. Broad sweeps and dense stands of low maintenance sabal palm, saw palmettos, macho and wart fern fill the understory space between the ground and the tree canopies. Local birds, butterflies and wildlife find an easy home here. Numerous huge staghorn and elkhorn ferns hang from the oaks and provide opportunities for the eye to marvel. The rear of the property features a gracious open lawn visible from porch and patio, providing a long green view and place for children to play.

Filtered light and the sound of breezes in the treetops are a constant in this enchanted setting, bringing shade and tranquility to its South Dade location. The palette of native trees and plants is in complete harmony with the architecture, creating a sense of peaceful and easy country living.

LEFT *Broad sweeps of saw palmetto and wart fern*
(Phymatosorus scolopendria) *provide textural interest
at the ground and shrub layers.*

ABOVE *A brick-edged gravel drive disappears into
dense vegetation.*

BELOW *The charming home is sheltered by stately Live oak, sabal or cabbage palm* (Sabal palmetto) *and saw palmetto* (Serenoa repens).

FACING TOP *A molasses cauldron, typical of sugar plantations, rests next to a hitching post.*

FACING MIDDLE *A sense of isolation is achieved with dense native vegetation from ground to canopy.*

FACING BELOW *The open canopy of the oaks allow wind and sunlight to filter through.*

TOP *A long bed of begonias between porch and walkway.*

MIDDLE *Rustic art and architecture among the textured trunks of sable palms.*

ABOVE *Brick fire pit surrounded by rockers in a corner of the garden.*

RIGHT *A giant Swiss cheese plant* (Monstera deliciosa) *lends an exotic note to a view of the rear lawn and patio.*

RIGHT
Living and entertaining are easy on the broad porch and brick patio in this carefree Low Country landscape.

BELOW LEFT
Open areas adjacent to wide, wrap-around porches funnel breezes to sitting areas.

BELOW RIGHT
Dappled sunlight plays upon the various greens of the landscape.

BELOW LEFT
The oak trees offer ideal conditions for hanging staghorn fern.

BELOW RIGHT
Occasional splashes of color from orchids and poinsettia punctuate the lush greenery.

Polynesian Inspiration on Biscayne Bay

THIS POLYNESIAN-STYLE ESCAPE on Miami Beach is the setting for a garden designed by Santi Diaz, where the lines between indoors and outdoors have been blurred, and water and light are central themes. The main house appears to sit within a large pool, drawing Biscayne Bay closer, and reflecting sky and palm trees from every angle. A feeling of almost total immersion in water combines with a panoramic view of Miami's skyline for a memorable experience.

The pool is the central feature, with a black pebble and mortar interior finish specially designed to enhance ever-changing reflections on the mirror-like surface. This oasis includes an elevated spa, deep water for swimming and safe shallows for wading. Stepping stones appear to float over the water, creating dry passage between deck and lawn. Narrow submerged walls permit short cuts across the expansive pool, while granting an uninterrupted reflective surface, and the remarkable visual experience of walking on water. A slightly raised water lily pond and fountain compliment the magnificent bay views from several rooms of the home.

Various garden rooms create gentle transitions from formal to casual, and from soothing to active spaces, with trickling fountains, reflecting pools, outdoor showers and sitting areas along the bay. An edible garden includes tropical fruits and vegetables, with herbs and spices for groundcover, fragrance and cooking.

Low Asian-inspired structures and a simple palette of warm wood, water, stone, glass and lush green foliage provide a soothing setting for a family for whom living gently and in harmony with the land is important.

The most magical moment of each day is when the sun sets over the reflecting pool and Miami's skyline is struck with an orange glow in the fading light. The pool blends into the bay, and the distant lights from PortMiami's cranes and the city lights create an astonishing light show.

ABOVE LEFT *Miami's dramatic skyline viewed across bay and pool.*

ABOVE *The large, multi-sectioned pool has a considerable span along the seawall. Elevated spa in foreground.*

ABOVE *A clump of five Phoenix sylvestris anchors the motor court.*

BOTTOM LEFT *Squared limestone pavers set a formal tone in the approach to the home.*

BOTTOM RIGHT *Irregular limestone pavers lead toward the casual play and relaxation areas.*

FACING ABOVE *Coconut palms, gamma grass and a patch of sand along the bay frontage lend a Polynesian feel.*

FACING BELOW *Shallow wading pools on the street side add to the feeling that the home is an island within an island.*

FOLLOWING TOP *The main pool wraps around the home and expansive deck.*

FOLLOWING BOTTOM LEFT *A quiet corner of the pool and deck near the master bedroom.*

FOLLOWING BOTTOM MIDDLE *A stone fire pit along the water's edge.*

FOLLOWING BOTTOM RIGHT *Pale stepping stone slabs contrast with the black-pebbled pool surfaces, appearing to float across the water.*

ABOVE *Inset lily pond and fountain basin within an alcove between wings of the home.*

RIGHT ABOVE *View across the fountain basin.*

RIGHT BELOW *The untreated lily pond water is separated from the swimming pool.*

FOLLOWING *The main pool mirrors the sky and trees and city skyline.*

GARDENS AND BOTANIC CENTERS

Miami-Dade County is fortunate to have a plethora of botanic gardens and horticultural research centers within its borders. Many are revered in the fields of horticulture and botanic research, as well as for their extensive plant collections. These gardens have served the regional community as places of inspiration, education and passive enjoyment for many decades. They have fueled awareness in such vast and diverse areas of study as palms, endangered and rare plants, tropical fruit, edible gardening, flowering trees, landscape design and native plant habitats.

Numerous owners, landscape architects and landscape designers, whose gardens are featured within the pages of this book, have drawn inspiration and collected plants from many of these places. They are important to our gardening history and have influenced the way we view our personal landscape spaces. The listing below includes the most renowned and influential. Each garden contains more detailed information on its website.

DEERING ESTATE AT CUTLER
16701 SW 72nd Avenue, Miami, FL 33157

The nearly 450 acres surrounding the Charles Deering Estate contain the Addison Hammock, an environmental, archaeological and natural preserve of considerable note, believed to contain the largest virgin coastal tropical hardwood hammock in the continental United States. It also contains globally endangered pine rockland habitat and mangrove forests.

The historic home is located on Biscayne Bay, along the original Old Cutler Trail. Deering resided here for only a few years until his death in the late 1920s. The State of Florida and Miami-Dade County purchased the property in 1985. Tours, educational programs, exhibits and myriad activities are available here, which are focused on the preservation of the natural habitat, as well as carrying on the traditions and innovative spirit of Charles Deering.

For more detailed information on this unique South Dade landmark, visit **deeringestate.com.**

FAIRCHILD TROPICAL BOTANIC GARDEN
10901 Old Cutler Road, Coral Gables, FL 33156

Founded in 1938, Fairchild's stated mission has been "exploring, explaining and conserving the world of tropical plants." Named for and influenced by David Fairchild, this 83-acre garden was actually founded by Colonel Robert H. Montgomery, Fairchild's friend and neighbor. The garden's history is long and fascinating, and its accolades are numerous and substantial. Its living collections, especially of palms and cycads, are world renowned.

While its reputation and reach is international, the influence of Fairchild Tropic Botanic Garden within our local gardening community cannot be overstated. This is a center of research, education, inspiration, community outreach and sharing. For the home enthusiast, annual Member Plant Sale events find people lining up long before opening to be able to purchase unusual and rare plants which are seldom found elsewhere, and appear in so many gardens found within this book.

For more information on Fairchild Tropical Botanic Garden, its many collections, exhibits, educational programs and events, please visit **fairchildgarden.org**.

Fruit and Spice Park
24801 SW 187th Avenue, Homestead, FL 33031

Founded in 1945 in the Redland, this 37-acre botanical garden and park contains over 500 varieties of fruit, vegetables, spices and herbs. It is the "go-to" destination for information on tropical fruit and edible gardening in southern Miami-Dade County, and the only tropical botanical garden of its kind in the United States.

There are over 160 varieties of mango and 75 varieties of bananas here alone, along with numerous other edible specimens from around the world. Visitors can tour the property, sample what is in season and learn about the wide world of tropical fruit. Membership and volunteer opportunities are available here along with a continuous calendar of events focused on education and entertainment.

Please visit **fruitandspicepark.org** for more information on this Redland gem.

John C. Gifford Arboretum, University of Miami

University of Miami, Coral Gables, FL 33146

Located within the northwestern quadrant of the main campus of the University of Miami, this arboretum and botanical garden was originally planted and founded in 1947. It was named for Professor John C. Gifford, an expert on, and a professor of, tropical forestry at UM. Over the years, its collections have grown and now number over 500 specimens of tropical plants and trees. The arboretum is run and maintained by the University of Miami's Department of Biology and the Friends of the Gifford Arboretum Committee. Guided tours and lectures are available throughout the year, as are horticultural workshops, plant sales and festivals.

Please visit **bio.miami.edu/arboretum** for a calendar, plot maps and more information on plant collections.

The Kampong
4013 Douglas Road, Coconut Grove, FL 33133

Located on 9 acres fronting Biscayne Bay in Coconut Grove, The Kampong became the beloved home of legendary horticulturist David Fairchild and his wife, Marian, in 1916. In March, 1984, The Kampong was gifted to the Hawaii-based National Tropical Botanical Garden (NTBG) by then property owner Catherine Sweeney. NTBG was established in 1969 by Congressional Charter in recognitiion of its national and public importance. The Kampong is now jointly managed by Florida International University and NTBG and will be home to the new International Center for Trioical Botany. Heritage collections from Central and South America, the Caribbean and Southeast Asia are found at The Kampong, including rare palms, flowering trees and tropical fruit cultivars. This enchanting and historic estate and garden hosts tours, eductaional programs and special events and serves as NTBG's mainland campus for botany and horticultural classes.

The Villagers have provided funding for the restoration of Dr. Fairchild's office, also on the grounds. More information can be found on their website, **ntbg.org/gardens/kampong.php**.

MIAMI BEACH BOTANICAL GARDEN
2000 Convention Center Drive, Miami Beach, FL 33139

The mission of the Miami Beach Botanical Garden is "to promote environmental enjoyment, stewardship and sustainability through education, the arts and interaction with the natural world." This 2.6-acre urban greenspace is owned by the City of Miami Beach and operated by the Miami Beach Garden Conservancy, a non-profit organization founded to restore the garden in the 1990s. It strives to be a hub for arts and cultural programming, environmental education and a resource for the community.

Visit **mbgarden.org** for details about the history, opportunities to volunteer and a calendar of events.

Montgomery Botanical Center
11901 Old Cutler Road, Coral Gables, FL 33156

Montgomery Botanical Center is widely known and respected in the fields of tropical botany and plant science. Preserving and displaying living specimens from wild plant populations from around the globe, this 120 acre nonprofit botanical garden is located in the southern portion of Coral Gables. Colonel Robert Montgomery established the live plant collections in 1932. The Colonel's wife, Nell Montgomery Jennings, established the Montgomery Botanical Center, originally known as the Montgomery Foundation, in 1959. The garden focuses its study on palms and cycads, with National Palm and Cycad Collections located here. Its mission is "to advance science, education, conservation, and horticultural knowledge of tropical plants…and to exemplify excellent botanical garden design."

While this is a center for scientific research, it is also a well-known resource in the community, which hosts lectures and workshops and provides tours of the plant collections to the public by appointment only.

For more information please visit their website at **montgomerybotanical.org**.

PINECREST GARDENS
11000 Red Road, Pinecrest, FL 33156

Pinecrest Gardens celebrates, cultivates and conserves the rich botanical heritage of South Florida. Its mission is to enrich the lives of its community through education, community service, historic preservation and the sustainable management of this public garden. It includes a botanical garden, a butterfly exhibit, a swan lake, children's playground and a splash and play area, providing an entertainment destination that fosters artistic excellence, diversity and a spirit of community.

Originally known as Parrot Jungle, the garden was created by an Austrian, Franz Scherr, in the 1930s, who envisioned an attraction where birds would "fly free." He rented 20 acres of hammock land and began creating a winding nature trail through the hammock, leaving the natural flora intact. The unique pitched roof entrance building was built on Red Road, and in December, 1936, the first visitors paid 25 cents to see the birds, trees and flowers. Over the years, the Parrot Jungle became a world-famous attraction, entertaining over one million visitors. In 2002, the attraction was moved to Miami's Watson Island and renamed Jungle Island. That same year, the young Village of Pinecrest purchased the Garden to serve as a municipal park. In 2011, it was added to the National Register of Historic Places. For detailed information, visit: **pinecrest-fl.gov**.

Vizcaya Museum and Gardens

3251 South Miami Avenue, Miami, FL 33129

Located along Biscayne Bay, this National Historic Landmark is also a beloved local treasure. The villa (completed in 1916) and formal gardens (completed in 1922) were created as the winter home of James Deering. The gardens are recognized as the premier example of a formal European garden in the United States. This public garden draws inspiration from classic traditions of French and Italian landscape design styles while using plant material compatible with Miami's sub-tropical heat and humidity.

Contained within the overall landscape design plan is a series of garden rooms that integrate within the larger whole. While the classic European garden relies on topography to "hide" and "reveal" distinct areas, this is accomplished at Vizcaya through the use of water features, statuary walls and other landscape devices. This technique is evident in a number of the larger private gardens featured in this book. It is also important to note that Deering preserved areas of subtropical forest, rockland hammock and mangroves on this property during its initial construction.

To read more about this historic property and its diverse horticultural collections, visit **vizcaya.org.**

GARDEN CLUBS AND PLANT SOCIETIES

The following is a list of garden-related organizations in Miami-Dade County. The information is subject to change since many are volunteer-driven. Always check websites, call or email to confirm meetings.

American Bamboo Society, Florida Caribbean Chapter: This group is dedicated to gaining knowledge and educating the public on bamboos, with emphasis on research, preservation and propagation of endangered species, and the uses of bamboo for construction, artistic and utilitarian applications. **www.tropicalbamboo.org**.

American Orchid Society: The society promotes and supports the passion for orchids through education, conservation and research. This is an 85-year old national organization headquartered at Fairchild Tropical Botanic Garden. **www.aos.org**.

The American Society of Landscape Architects, Florida Chapter, Miami Section: This professional organization represents members in Monroe and Miami-Dade Counties, providing professional, educational, service and social activities for members. **www.flasla.org**

Bonsai Society of Miami: This organization's goal is to advance the education of its members and the general public in the aesthetic, historical, scientific, business and social features of the art of bonsai. It meets on the fourth Wednesday at 7:30 PM at Pinecrest Gardens. **www.bonsaisocietyofmiami.org**.

Bromeliad Society of South Florida: This group presents speakers who conduct informative talks about bromeliads. The group meets on the third Tuesday at 7:30 PM at Fairchild Tropical Botanic Garden. **www.timewolf.net/BSSF**.

Caribbean Basin African Violet and Gesneriad Society: This society is devoted to the identification, culture, propagation and conservation of gesneriad species and cultivars. Meetings are held the second Saturday from 10:00 AM until noon, at Palm Hammock Orchid Estate, 9995 SW 66 St., Miami. **www.gesneriadsociety.org**.

Coconut Grove Garden Club: Projects of the club include planting gardens with Slow Food Miami at schools, tending gardens at the Barnacle, and planting trees with Treemendous Miami. The Club meets in members' homes and other locations in the Coconut Grove area. **www.coconutgrovegardenclub.jimbo.com**.

Coral Gables Garden Club: The club is dedicated to studying horticulture and the artistic use of plant materials and offering opportunities to learn about conservation and gardening. Meetings are held on the fourth Monday, Sept. through May, usually at the Biltmore Hotel. **www.coralgablesgardenclub.org**.

Dadeland Garden Club: The club meets the second Thursday, Sept. through May. For information, contact: **ffgc.wildapricot.org**.

Coral Pines Garden Club: The club meets on the second Monday, Sept. through May. For information, contact: **ffgc.wildapricot.org**.

East Everglades Orchid Society: The purpose is to educate members and the public in the classification, evolution, propagation, culture, care and development of orchids and to support their conservation. It meets the fourth Tuesday of the month, with a mini-class at 7:15 PM and the general meeting at 8 PM, University of Florida Miami-Dade County Extension Building, 18710 SW 288th Street, Homestead. **www.orchidseeos.com**.

Florida Federation of Garden Clubs: The mission is to further the education of the members and the public in the fields of gardening, horticulture, botany, floral design, landscape design, environmental awareness through the conservation of natural resources, civic beautification, nature studies, and to instill in our youth the love of gardening and the respect and protection of the environment. **www.ffgc.org**.

Florida Native Plant Society for Miami-Dade County and the Florida Keys: The purpose is to promote the preservation, conservation and restoration of the native plants and native plant communities of Florida, and the use of Florida native plants in landscaping. It meets at 7:30 PM at Pinecrest Gardens on the last Tuesday. **www.dade.fnpschapters.org**.

Florida Nursery, Growers and Landscape Association: The mission is to promote and protect the success and professionalism of members. The Dade County Office is at 18710 SW 288 St., #38, Homestead, FL 33030. **www.fngla.org/ chapters/Dade**.

Friends of the Fruit and Spice Park: Tropical Fruit and Vegetable Society of the Redland: The objective is to increase public interest in the cultivation and use of tropical fruit and vegetables in South Florida, and to support the Fruit and Spice Park through volunteer efforts and donations. Meetings are the last Wednesday at 7:30 PM at the Fruit and Spice Park. **fruitandspicepark.org**

Garden Club at Miami Veterans Medical Center: This is a horticultural therapy program for the VAMC Nursing Home. The group meets 3 times a week. **www.va_garden_club.tripod.com**.

Ikebana International Miami: The group objectives are to stimulate, cultivate and perpetuate the study of Ikebana related arts and culture throughout the world. Meetings are held on the third Tuesday of the months Sept. to Nov. and Jan. to April, at Fairchild Botanic Tropical Garden beginning at 9:30 AM. **www.ikebanamiami.org**.

International Aroid Society: The society supports aroid education, research, and horticulture through publications, awards, events and the website. **www.aroid.org/society**.

Ken Pines Garden Club: Meets the second Wednesday, Sept. through May. For information, contact: **ffgc.wildapricot.org**.

Miami Beach Garden Club: The mission is to promote the cultivation of plants and flowers in the community through projects that focus on beautification of the city, mentoring and sponsoring student programs and support of the Miami Beach Botanical Garden. It meets the second Thursday, October through May, at the Miami Beach Botanical Garden. **www.miamibeachgardenclub.com**.

Miami Blue Chapter, North American Butterfly Association: This group provides information on plants that attract butterflies and has an annual butterfly count. **www.miamiblue.org**.

Miami Lakes Garden Club: The club objective is to encourage civic beauty, to stimulate interest among the amateur gardeners and to study all aspects of the art of gardening. It meets the fourth Monday, Sept. through May. **www.miamilakesgardenclub.com.**

Miami Rare Fruit Council International: The organization is dedicated to the education, introduction and promotion of rare tropical fruits. The group meets on the second Wednesday at 7:30 PM in the Science Village Auditorium at Fairchild Tropical Botanic Garden. Programs have guest speakers, a tasting table of exotic fruits, plant and seed exchanges. **www.tropicalfruitnews.org.**

North Dade Orchid Club: A group for persons who love orchids and want to learn about growing these plants. The group meets on the fourth Monday of every month except May, Nov., and Dec. at the McDonald Center, 17051 NE 19 Ave, North Miami Beach, at 7:00 PM. **www.northdadeorchidclub.webs.com.**

Orchid Society of Coral Gables: The purpose is to educate members in the finer points of good orchid culture, exhibition and orchid conservation. This group is an affiliate of the American Orchid Society. Meetings are on the first Tuesday in the Garden Room of Fairchild Tropical Botanic Garden with a beginners' class at 6:45 and the meeting at 7:30 PM. **www.oscgonline.org.**

Palmetto Bay Garden Club: A group for residents interested in gardening. Meetings are held on the fourth Tuesday at 7 PM on the second floor of the Feller Community Center located at the Palmetto Bay Branch Library, 17641 Old Cutler Road. **www.palmettobaygreen.com.**

Pan American Orchid Society: Founded by Pan American World Airways employees to share knowledge and love of orchids. This group meets every third Tuesday at Pinecrest Gardens Hibiscus Room. **www.paos09.wordpress.com.**

Pinecrest Garden Club: The club goal is to encourage good landscaping of homes and grounds in the Pinecrest community; to strive for excellence in the practice of horticulture; to encourage development of talent in artistic design, and to stimulate interest in environment and ecology. The club meets on the second Tuesday at 11:30 AM in the Hibiscus Room of Pinecrest Gardens. **www.pinecrestgardenclub.com.**

Redland Evening Herb Society: Meetings share how to grow herbs and what to grow for your health, cooking or crafts. Members provide volunteer assistance at the Fruit and Spice Park during special events and festivals. Meetings are the first Wednesday of every month at the Fruit and Spice Park. **www.fruitandspicepark.org.**

Shenandoah Garden Club: The club meets the first Wednesday, Oct. through May.

Slow Food Miami: This organization does plantings to encourage the enjoyment of foods that are local, seasonal and sustainably grown. **events@slowfoodmiami.org.**

South Dade Garden Club: Meets second Thursday all year at 7:00 PM, Fruit and Spice Park. Information, contact: **ffgc.wildapricot.org.**
South Miami Garden Club: The club promotes mutual helpfulness among members in the study of practical gardening, to promote ex-

cellence in horticulture, to inspire public interest in landscape art and to protect and conserve the natural resources of South Florida. Meetings are the first Tuesday, Sept. through May, in members' homes. **keyeslm@bellsouth.net**

South Florida Cactus and Succulent Society, Inc. The purpose is to promote education and cooperation among those interested in the study, culture, and propagation of cacti and succulents. Meets quarterly. **www.sfloridacactus.org.**

South Florida Palm Society: The purpose is to disseminate information and encourage interest in palms and the use of those plants. Meets in the Garden House at Fairchild Tropical Botanic Garden, at 7:30 PM on the first Monday of even months: Feb., April, June, Aug., Oct., and Dec. **www.southfloridapalmsociety.org**

Sunset Park Garden Club: The club meets on the second Thursday, Sept. through May. For information, contact: **ffgc.wildapricot.org.**

Town and Country Garden Club: Meets the first Thursday, Sept. through May. For information, contact: **ffgc.wildapricot.org.**

Treemendous Miami: Promoting and preserving trees in Miami-Dade County. **www.treemendousmiami.org.**

Tropical Fern and Exotic Plant Society: The group is for persons interested in ferns, begonias, aroids, bromeliads, heliconias, and hibiscus. Meetings are held at Fairchild Tropical Botanic Garden on the fourth Monday, Sept. through June. **www.tfeps.org.**

Tropical Flowering Tree Society: The goals of the society include sharing knowledge, preservation and distribution of tropical flowering trees. The society meets on the second Monday at 7:30 PM at Fairchild Tropical Botanic Garden, except for May, July and August. The Royal Poinciana Fiesta is sponsored by the society, as well as an annual flowering tree show and sale. **www.tfts.org.**

Tropical Rose Society of Greater Miami: This group is dedicated to enlightening members and the general public about growing roses and rose culture. Meets at Fairchild Tropical Botanic Garden on the third Tuesday in Jan., Feb., Mar., May, Sept., Oct., and Nov. **www.tropicalrose.org.**

University of Florida/Miami-Dade County Extension Service: This agency focuses on educational outreach through workshops, seminars, demonstrations, educational materials and mass media. County Extension Director, 18710 SW 288 ST., Homestead, FL 33030, 305-248-3311. **dade@ifas.ulf.edu.**